Strategic Studies Institute
and
U.S. Army War College Press

THE CHINESE PEOPLE'S LIBERATION ARMY AND INFORMATION WARFARE

Larry M. Wortzel

March 2014

*****

Comments pertaining to this report are invited and should be forwarded to: Director, Strategic Studies Institute and U.S. Army War College Press, U.S. Army War College, 47 Ashburn Drive, Carlisle, PA 17013-5010.

*****

*****

FOREWORD

On November 23, 2013, China's Ministry of National Defense spokesman announced that a new air defense intercept zone (ADIZ) will be established by the government to include the Diaoyu, or Senkaku Islands. Sovereignty over these islands is disputed by Japan, China, and Taiwan. The new ADIZ also included a submerged rock that falls inside overlapping Exclusive Economic Zones (EEZ) claimed by China, Japan, and South Korea. Pundits and policy analysts quickly engaged in a broad debate about whether China's expanded ADIZ is designed to create tension in Asia, or is part of a broader plan to impose a new definition of China's territorial space in the Asia-Pacific region. Meanwhile, to deal with cyber penetrations attributed to the Chinese People's Liberation Army (PLA), the U.S. Departments of Justice, Homeland Security, and State are devising new means to protect intellectual property and secrets from the PLA's computer network operations.

Dr. Larry M. Wortzel's monograph puts these events into perspective. The ADIZ announcement by China, at one level, is an example of the PLA General Political Department engagement in what it calls "legal warfare," part of the PLA's "three warfares." In expanding its ADIZ, China is stretching International Civil Aviation Organization regulations to reinforce its territorial claims over the Senkaku Islands, administered by Japan. China calls these the Diaoyu Islands and, along with Taiwan, claims them for its own. On another level, the Chinese government will use the ADIZ as a way to increase the airspace it can monitor and control off its coast; it already is suing the navy and maritime law enforcement ships to enforce these claims at sea. Additionally, the PLA and the Chinese government have sent a major signal to Taiwan, demonstrating another aspect of the "three warfares." When the Chinese Ministry of National Defense put its expanded ADIZ into effect, the new zone carefully avoided any infringement into Taiwan's ADIZ, signaling that in addition to the improved economic ties with Taiwan, there is room for political improvement across the Taiwan Strait.

The PLA spent more than a decade examining U.S. military publications on network-centric warfare and the evolution of American doctrine on information warfare. After observing American information operations in the Balkans and the first Gulf War, the PLA saw the effect of modern information operations on the battlefield and in the international arena. The PLA then began to implement its own form of information warfare. The Chinese military has adopted information warfare concepts suited to its own organization and doctrine, blending its own traditional tactics, concepts from the Soviet military, and U.S. doctrine to bring the PLA into the information age. At the same time, the PLA has modernized and improved upon its own psychological warfare operations and expanded the role for its legal scholars in justifying military action and territorial claims.

The PLA's command, control, communications, computers, intelligence, surveillance, and reconnaissance programs support the ground forces, navy, air force, missile forces, nuclear doctrine, and space warfare. China's military doctrine depends on incorporating information technology and networked information operations. The PLA's operational concepts for employing traditional signals intelligence and electronic warfare have expanded to include cyber warfare; kinetic and cyber attacks on satellites; and information confrontation operations across the electromagnetic spectrum. In doing so, as Dr. Wortzel's monograph explains, the PLA used innovative means to expand on Cold War Soviet doctrine on "radio-electronic combat," which called for a combination of jamming and precision air, missile and artillery strikes on North Atlantic Treaty Organization forces. The Chinese military, however, apparently intends to conduct these activities at the tactical, operational and strategic levels of war, envisioning attacks on an enemy's homeland critical infrastructure and points of embarkation.

Along with these more technical aspects of information operations, the PLA's combination of psychological warfare; the manipulation of public opinion, or media warfare; and the manipulation of legal arguments to strengthen China's diplomatic and security position—or what China calls "legal warfare"—join together in a comprehensive information operations doctrine. This monograph explains how the PLA is revising its operational doctrine to meet what it sees as the new mode of "integrated, joint operations" for the 21st century. An understanding of thee PLA's new concepts are important for U.S. and allied military leaders and planners.

DOUGLAS C. LOVELACE, JR.
Director
Strategic Studies Institute and
    U.S. Army War College Press

ABOUT THE AUTHOR

LARRY M. WORTZEL is a retired U.S. Army colonel who spent much of his career in the Asia-Pacific region. He is a commissioner on the U.S.-China Economic and Security Review Commission. After 3 years as a U.S. Marine, he joined the Army and trained in Mandarin Chinese. He was assigned as a signals intelligence collector in northeast Thailand for the Army Security Agency. He was commissioned in the infantry in 1973, and transferred to military intelligence in 1977. He served as assistant Army attaché in China from 1988 to 1990 and was Army attaché in China from 1995 to 1997. Dr. Wortzel was director of the Strategic Studies Institute at the U.S. Army War College from 1997 to 1999. After retiring from the military, he served as Asian studies director and vice president at The Heritage Foundation. He has written or edited 11 books about China, as well as numerous policy papers and journal articles. This monograph is developed from his latest book, *The Dragon Extends its Reach: Chinese Military Power Goes Global* (Potomac Books, Inc., 2013). Dr. Wortzel is a graduate of the Armed Forces Staff College and the U.S. Army War College, and holds a Ph.D. from the University of Hawaii.

SUMMARY

On November 23, 2013, China's Ministry of National Defense spokesman announced that a new air defense intercept zone (ADIZ) will be established by the government to include the Diaoyu, or Senkaku Islands. Sovereignty over these islands is disputed by Japan, China, and Taiwan. Pundits and policy analysts quickly engaged in a broad debate about whether China's expanded ADIZ is designed to create tension in Asia, or is part of a broader plan to impose a new definition of China's territorial space in the Asia-Pacific region. Meanwhile, to deal with cyber penetrations attributed to the Chinese People's Liberation Army (PLA), the U.S. Departments of Justice, Homeland Security, and State are devising new means to protect intellectual property and secrets from the PLA's computer network operations.

The ADIZ announcement by China is an example of the PLA General Political Department engagement in what it calls "legal warfare," part of the PLA's "three warfares." In expanding its ADIZ, China is stretching International Civil Aviation Organization regulations to reinforce its territorial claims over the Senkaku Islands. On another level, the Chinese government will use the ADIZ as a way to increase the airspace it can monitor and control off its coast; the Chinese government is already suing the navy and maritime law enforcement ships to enforce these claims at sea. Additionally, the PLA and the Chinese government have sent a major signal to Taiwan, demonstrating another aspect of the "three warfares." When the Chinese Ministry of National Defense put its expanded ADIZ into effect, the new zone carefully avoided any infringement into Taiwan's ADIZ, signaling that in addition to the improved economic ties with Taiwan, there is room for political improvement across the Taiwan Strait.

The PLA spent more than a decade examining U.S. military publications on network-centric warfare and the evolution of American doctrine on information warfare. After observing American information operations in the Balkans and the first Gulf War, the PLA saw the effect of modern information operations on the battlefield and in the international arena. The PLA then began to implement its own form of information warfare. The Chinese military has adopted information warfare concepts suited to its own organization and doctrine—blending its own traditional tactics, concepts from the Soviet military, and U.S. doctrine to bring the PLA into the information age. At the same time, the PLA has modernized and improved upon its own psychological warfare operations and expanded the role of its legal scholars in justifying military action and territorial claims.

The PLA's command, control, communications, computers, intelligence, surveillance, and reconnaissance programs support the ground forces, navy, air force, missile forces, nuclear doctrine, and space warfare. China's military doctrine depends on incorporating information technology and networked information operations. The PLA's operational concepts for employing traditional signals intelligence and electronic warfare have expanded to include cyber warfare; kinetic and cyber attacks on satellites; and information confrontation operations across the electromagnetic spectrum. As this monograph explains, the PLA used innovative means to expand on Cold War Soviet doctrine on "radio-electronic combat," which called for a combination of jamming and precision air, missile, and artillery strikes on North Atlantic Treaty Organization forces. The Chinese military, however, apparently intends to conduct these activities at the tactical, operational, and strategic levels of war, envisioning attacks on an enemy's homeland critical infrastructure and points of embarkation.

Along with these more technical aspects of information operations, the PLA's combination of psychological warfare; the manipulation of public opinion, or media warfare; and the manipulation of legal arguments to strengthen China's diplomatic and security position, or what China calls "legal warfare," join together in a comprehensive information operations doctrine. This monograph explains how the PLA is revising its operational doctrine to meet what it sees as the new mode of "integrated, joint operations" for the 21st century. An understanding of the PLA's new concepts is important for U.S. and allied military leaders and planners.

THE CHINESE PEOPLE'S LIBERATION ARMY AND INFORMATION WARFARE[1]

CHINA'S MILITARY IMPLEMENTS INFORMATION OPERATIONS

The Chinese People's Liberation Army (PLA) spent a decade or so examining U.S. military publications on network-centric warfare and the evolution of American doctrine on information warfare. For a while, this was an all new and interesting theory to the PLA, but after observing American information operations in the Balkans and the first Gulf War, the PLA saw the effect of modern information operations on the battlefield and in the international arena. The PLA then began to implement its own form of information warfare. Over a 20-year period, the Chinese military has adopted information warfare concepts suited to its own organization and doctrine — blending its own traditional tactics, concepts from the Soviet military, and U.S. doctrine to bring the PLA into the information age.

The PLA's command, control, communications, computers, intelligence, surveillance, and reconnaissance (C4ISR) programs support the ground forces, navy, air force, missile forces, nuclear doctrine, and space warfare. China's military doctrine depends on incorporating information technology and networked information operations. The PLA's warfighting concepts for employing signals intelligence and electronic warfare have expanded to include cyber warfare, attacks on satellites, and information confrontation operations (*xinxi duikang zuozhan*).[2] Along with these more technical aspects of information operations, the PLA's combination of psychological warfare; the

1

manipulation of public opinion, or media warfare; and the manipulation of legal arguments to strengthen China's diplomatic and security position, or what China calls "legal warfare," join together in a comprehensive information operations doctrine.

INFORMATION AGE WARFARE AND INTEGRATED NETWORK ELECTRONIC WARFARE

In modern military operations, it is nearly impossible to find forms of military activity that do not in some way depend on information technology. Navigation and positioning is no longer done with compasses or sextants, maps, or charts; it is done with satellite broadcasts. Physical reconnaissance is complemented by electronic means and a range of sensors employed on land or in the in air, sea, and space. Information systems support logistics activities, such as resupply and refueling, and facilitate personnel and casualty management. Information technology and instantaneous data exchange provide commanders and deployed forces with a shared awareness of the battle area. In most military organizations, units that were engaged in signals intelligence collection and electronic warfare also have taken on the mission of cyber warfare and cyber penetration.

During World War II and into the Cold War, opposing forces used electronic warfare techniques such as jamming, imitative communications deception, and meaconing (the interception, alteration, and rebroacasting of navigation signals) to disrupt an adversary's communication system and radar or to alter electromagnetic signals. In the information age, similar actions are possible, and cyber exploitation or attacks can supplement electronic warfare. This matters because operational concepts such as cooperative target engagement—in which different combat platforms in the air, on the sea, on land, or on submarine share data on a target and fire at it simultaneously from various directions with different weapons—are based on information systems being linked. These linkages, however, also create opportunities for systems-wide attacks.

For the PLA, information warfare is directed at "the enemy's information detection sources, information channels, and information-processing and decision making systems."[3] The goals are information superiority, disruption of the enemy information control capabilities, and maintaining one's own information systems and capabilities.

In the age of information operations, militaries that embrace information systems have begun to think about information dominance, or the ability to identify a range of threats against their own forces; to counter them; and to attack the enemy's information systems.[4] The PLA is working to create an information-based "system of systems operations capability that forms an all-inclusive master network."[5] This effort depends on the redundant national command-and-control architecture that the PLA began to develop in the 1990s. In July 1997, at an exhibition in the PLA Military History Museum in Beijing, the author observed an overlay for a national and theater-level automated command-and-control system.

The PLA's national command-and-control system is a redundant military region or theater of war networked system linking the General Staff Department headquarters and the PLA's arms and services with regional combat headquarters and their subordinate

3

major organizations. An Indian defense researcher described this *Qu Dian* system as using fiberoptic cable, high-frequency and very-high-frequency communications, microwave systems, and multiple satellites to enable the Central Military Commission, the General Staff Department, and commanders to communicate with forces in their theater of war on a real-time basis.[6] The system also permits data transfer among the headquarters and all the units under the PLA's joint command.

Leaders and military strategists in the PLA observed the transformation taking place in American and other Western military forces and worked hard to understand what was happening. The Chinese military moved steadily to take advantage of information technologies.[7] In a New Year's Day 2006 editorial, the *PLA Daily* reminded the armed forces to transform itself from a force that operates under mechanized conditions to one that operates under "informatized conditions."[8] Less than a month before this reminder, in a testimonial to Hu Jintao's speech on the historic missions of the PLA, *PLA Daily* made it clear that the military had to "improve integrated combat operations capabilities under informatized conditions."[9]

A range of military activities depends on how information technologies make military units and systems "interconnected." But the PLA still is not fully able to connect various command posts at different levels of the military to the national level and to each other. Nor are all the arms and services of the PLA fully interconnected yet. The PLA's goal is to create a "system of systems in operations" (*ti xi zuozhan*) that can coordinate activities across the military inside and between military regions, arms, and services.[10] One objective of the effort is to develop a networked

4

command-and-control system inside the PLA at the tactical, operational, and strategic levels of war, ultimately extending from the national command level to the soldier.[11] It is clear, however, that China's military ultimately envisions an information system or complex that can ensure that reconnaissance, electronic warfare, cyber systems, and combat strikes are integrated.[12]

In their book, *The Science of Military Strategy*, Peng Guangqian and Yao Yunzhu highlight the effectiveness of precision-guided weapons and information age technologies. They note that in the Gulf War, which depended a great deal on information systems, "precision-guided weapons made up only 7 percent of all weapons used by the U.S. military, but they destroyed 80 percent of important targets."[13] Further, Peng and Yao argue that "under high tech conditions, the outcome of war not only depends on the amount of resources, manpower and technology devoted to the battlefield," but also on "the control of information on the battlefield." Battle effectiveness, they maintain, is a function of the acquisition, transmission, and management of information.[14]

The PLA, however, moved into the information age from a less advantageous position than did the United States. For decades, military culture in China emphasized the importance of people, not equipment, in warfare and employed massed forces or weapons—the strengths China brought to bear in the Korean War, the Sino-Indian War, and the Sino-Vietnam War.[15] Although the PLA had electronic systems, it did not modernize a force with the intent to use and even depend on these systems. The educational base of the average soldier in the PLA is probably lower than that of American or European soldiers, and the same is still true of many PLA officers.

At all levels of the PLA, however, attitudes about the relative importance of technology in warfare are changing. As China's military moves into the second decade of the 21st century, it is embracing the information age. The PLA is updating 20th-century mechanized and joint operations, and combining them with electronic warfare, warfare — what the PLA calls "firepower warfare" — and precision strike. In a book published by the PLA Academy of Military Science, Ye Zheng describes information age operations as "a new type of operations that are derived from the basis of mechanized operations moving from 'platform-based operations' to systematic operations and network-centric operations."[16]

Even though some PLA theorists argue that "the next 20 years are a period for China's 'peaceful rise,' meaning that China should not threaten others," this does not mean that China cannot be prepared to defend itself from aggression.[17] Further, information age warfare involves the Global Information Grid, a term the U.S. National Security Agency uses to describe "interconnected, end-to-end set of information capabilities for collecting, processing, storing, disseminating and managing" information for warfighters and policymakers.[18] For the PLA, this means connecting global command-and-control systems and global positioning satellites to provide data for strategic operations and theaters of war.[19] Ultimately, however, PLA theorists acknowledge that warfare is about killing and destruction, "just as mechanization in war made war more destructive, information age warfare will allow fires to be more destructive."[20]

First "Informatize," then Network.

Setting the tone for wider implementation of the PLA's "informatization," the General Staff Department explains that the process will be both long and dynamic.[21] The PLA must embrace information age operations in support of all forms of military operations: in creating space-, ground-, and service-based system networks by integrating electronic systems in military regions, and by establishing effective command organizations and structures that will "possess powerful capabilities with regard to mobile suppression of the enemy [*jidong zhi di*], long-range strikes [*yuancheng daji*], precisions support [*jingque baozhang*], and three-dimensional defense [*quawei fanghu*]."[22]

Space-based information networks are described as the "backbone" of any informatization effort for the PLA. Surface-based systems are the key elements of the effort, supported by air and sea platforms, and the "integrated ground air and space elements must be compatible with the various services and their surrounding regions."[23] The PLA also is concerned about such matters as bandwidth, which is the basis for the ability to support a high volume of transmissions and system survivability and to confront enemy information systems.[24]

An article in *PLA Daily* emphasized that today we are all living on a "smart planet," which is interconnected, with economic, political, and cultural activities all available to see on information systems — allowing military forces to take advantage of this transparency on the battlefield.[25] PLA strategists argue that "battlespace awareness is the core of information age warfare," which means that one's forces must be able to destroy or jam the adversary's systems that are fundamental to situational awareness. Given this, PLA experts believe that "information age warfare will take place in a range of strategic battle-space: land, maritime, air, space, and 'knowledge areas'."[26]

Using the same formula for decisionmaking in the information age relied on by the U.S. Armed Forces, Ye Zheng tells the PLA that the interaction of systems, platforms, communications, and decisions shortens the "OODA [observe, orient, decide, and act, or *faxian, juece, jihua, xingdong*] loop," allowing a military to take action in real time.[27] Moreover, as he explains, in information operations the traditional concepts of air, land, and sea battlespace expand to include the electromagnetic spectrum, cyberspace, and space, becoming "virtual battle space" (*xu kong jian*).[28] The PLA defines this as "the space created by technology, computers and the 'web' [Internet] that is subject to human control and reflects human will."[29] Its components are cyberspace (*saibo kongjian*), information space (*xinsi kongjian*), and digital space (*shuxue kongjian*).

The truly distinguishing characteristic of operations in the information age in PLA doctrine, however, is that "information power and various types of firepower are merged" so that mobility and precision fires are integrated to increase their operational effects.[30] Ultimately, the PLA must execute integrated operations combining computer network warfare, networked firepower warfare, electronic warfare, and sensor systems.

Part of the dilemma for the PLA, however, is to develop new cyber warfare doctrine appropriate for the PLA's level of modernization, while at the same time taking advantage of the Chinese armed forces' existing strengths in electronic warfare, electronic information gathering, precision attack, and massed firepower.[31]

The PLA also lacks a deep reservoir of personnel who can manage or operate such systems. Chinese military leaders, however, recognize this weakness and intend to develop a talent pool of troops who can conduct or plan joint military operations, manage information systems and cyber technology, and use or maintain advanced weapon systems.[32] The PLA's goal is to have these personnel by 2020.

However, the degree to which individual units or combat platforms are truly integrated into a data-sharing and command system varies in the PLA by service, branch, and arm. In major ground formations (infantry, armor, artillery), few units are networked below the regimental level. In the PLA Navy (PLAN), the majority of surface combatants and submarines have the communications and data-sharing capabilities to be networked, as do PLA Air Force (PLAAF) combat and support aircraft and Second Artillery Corps missile-firing battalions. By comparison, in the U.S. military, the networked C4ISR system extends to every major combat platform and organization — often down to the rifle squad or individual combat vehicle. All aircraft and ships are in the networked system.

The GSD Communications Department calls for establishing five major networked systems:

1. Theater-level joint operational command communications and liaison subsystems that will synchronize broadband, multimedia information transmission.

2. Integrated processing subsystems for the operational command services such as message processing, mapping, simulations, and automated decisionmaking for peacetime, exercises, and wartime.

3. Fixed and mobile or portable theater reconnaissance and detection systems to improve intelligence,

reconnaissance, detection, information processing, and the rapid relay of such information to other defense posts, ports, stations, and substations. These should be able to cover four levels of units: military regions, group army-level organizations, divisions or brigades, and regiments. They should include such arms as air defense and missile units.

4. Electronic countermeasures and intelligence database systems that can integrate and share electromagnetic intelligence among headquarters, service arms in a theater of war, command posts at different levels, and reconnaissance stations.

5. Theater subsystems for political work operations, logistics, equipment monitoring, managing information systems, and managing theater-level intelligence-integrated processing systems.[33]

The Communications Department, however, anticipates challenges in reaching its goals. One problem is that the PLA cannot include units at the lower echelons in its communication and data exchange information networks. For the ground forces, in 2004, the information network extended only to the regimental level. By 2013, battalion command posts seem to be included in the network. The PLA wants to integrate information attack, attacks on enemy C4ISR systems, and precision strikes in "integrated network electronic warfare [INEW]," discussed later in this monograph.[34]

In *An Introduction to Informationalized Operations*, Ye Zheng explains that the PLA concept of informationalized operations means "networked firepower warfare employed across the domains of war."[35] The Chinese military realizes that integrated network electronic warfare attacks must be combined with integrated firepower warfare. This use of precision fires includes beyond-visual-range fires.[36]

To a great extent, when one analyzes the PLA's INEW doctrine, it is similar to the concept of radio-electronic combat (REC) in Cold War-Soviet military doctrine.[37] China's military, however, has added additional dimensions to this older concept. Taking a cue from U.S. operations in Iraq and the Balkans, China has moved beyond the tactical and theater realm of operations to elevate integrated network electronic warfare to a strategic level of war. Also, the PLA has added cyber attacks and attacks on satellites, or space warfare, to its offensive operations. Dai Qingmin envisions future combat operations focusing on "the destruction and control of the enemy's information infrastructure and strategic life blood, selecting key enemy targets, and launching effective network-electronic attacks."[38] In doing so, the PLA expects to weaken and paralyze an enemy's decisionmaking and also to weaken and paralyze the political, economic, and military aspects of the enemy's entire war potential. This suggests that INEW operations would take place within a theater of war but would also extend to an enemy's homeland, including the civil infrastructure and the economy.[39]

The concepts applied by the PLA are derivatives of both Soviet and American doctrine, as discussed earlier. A major contribution from U.S. doctrine resulted from the PLA's research into the U.S. Navy's writings about network-centric warfare.[40]

One American researcher characterizes the PLA's efforts at information age warfare as "a focused transformation of the nation's mode of thinking" to integrate traditional and mechanized military operations into a "systems-oriented environment characterized by rapidly changing time-space relationships."[41] Just as INEW theory seems to have evolved from Chinese research into Soviet military doctrine, the PLA's ideas on expanding REC to include information operations and space attacks were based on observations by China's military thinkers of U.S. and allied operations in Iraq and Kosovo.[42]

This mode of thinking involved maintaining information superiority over an adversary; integrating air, ground, and naval warfare; and taking "command and control of forces as a major part of military science."[43] In essence, for the PLA, the information and communication networks of engaged forces became the focal point for the conduct of military operations, as well as for finding and engaging enemy forces. Wang Zhengde conceived it as "merging weapons, equipment, resources, operational structure, and information resources to enable operational troops to truly form a grand system that fully exploits overall effectiveness."[44]

If we take Wang's embrace of information warfare concepts as a barometer of how the PLA approached the concept, by 2007 the threads of integrated network electronic warfare begin to emerge. In the book, *On Informationalized Confrontation*, he explores warfare (or military confrontation) in the electronic realm (*dianzi lingyu duikang*). Wang argues that "both sides in any conflict want control of the electromagnetic spectrum," making jamming and electronic countermeasures critical parts of military operations.[45] Further, as the PLA and other militaries evolve in the information age and come to depend on networks, the PLA's effort at informationalized confrontation evolves into "network confrontation operations," in which each side in a conflict is seeking to immobilize the other's communications, data, command, and sensor networks.[46]

INEW, Computer Network Warfare, and Strike.

One way to understand what the PLA is doing to expand and modernize what it learned is to think of Soviet REC on Chinese steroids. That is, by combining electronic warfare and precision strikes and adding cyber warfare and attacks on space systems, the PLA believes it can improve operational success on the modern battlefield.[47]

China's military strategists expand the Soviet concept further. Whereas the Soviet military applied REC to tactical situations in a limited battlespace or within a theater of operations, such as Europe, PLA military theorists introduce strategic attacks on an adversary's homeland sustainment and supply systems. This new doctrine, as China's armed forces envision it, extends across all levels of warfare, from the tactical battlefield to the theater of operations and to the strategic level of war. None of these effects can be achieved without the PLA realizing its objectives in integrated, or networked, operations.[48]

China's military researchers are aware of the Soviet REC doctrine and acknowledge the goals that the Soviet military set for REC.[49] In conceiving the REC concept during the Cold War, the Soviets expected their forces would inflict 60-percent casualties or combat damage on enemy forces through a combination of traditional electronic warfare and combat strikes by aircraft, helicopters, missiles, rockets, and artillery in the opening moves of any conflict.[50] The Soviet military goal was to destroy "30 percent by jamming and 30 percent by destructive fires."[51] The U.S. Army described REC as "the total integration of EW [electronic warfare] and physical destruction resources to deny us the use of our electronic systems."[52] Chinese researchers imply that in the information age, by adding in cyber warfare and attacks on space systems, the PLA can improve on the Soviet casualty ratios, even if they do not give specific numbers.[53]

Soviet REC was part of a broader operational campaign. Soviet forces intended to employ radio-direction finding, signals and radar intercept, and artillery radars to attack U.S. troop formations and headquarters—in addition to electronic systems to support strikes by artillery, combat aircraft, helicopters, and rockets or missiles. Among some of the measures included in Soviet REC operations were suppressive fires, jamming an adversary's communications assets, deceptively entering an adversary's radio nets, and interfering with the normal flow of an adversary's communications.[54]

Starting in the 1970s, the American response to Soviet doctrine, in the event of war in Europe, was AirLand Battle, an integrated attack plan using airpower, special operations forces, artillery, armor, and electronic warfare.[55] The United States also employed AirLand Battle doctrine in the Gulf War during the campaign to drive the Iraqi forces out of Kuwait, a campaign that the PLA studied with intense interest.[56]

Ultimately, the PLA rolled all these concepts into what it now terms "integrated network electronic warfare," or INEW. On the information systems side of China's INEW planning, Ye Zheng discusses integrated network information attack (*wangdian yiti xinxi gongji*) as integrating electronic warfare and computer warfare to destroy the enemy's information systems and to preserve one's own.[57] Other PLA operations experts, however, expand the concept to include attacking and destroying enemy equipment and personnel,

14

bringing the PLA's doctrine in line with the way that the Soviet Union conceived REC doctrine.

Chinese military thinkers built on the American concept of network-centric warfare to introduce concepts such as precision weapon strikes and the use of space-based and battlefield sensors with the goal of moving away from what one Chinese strategist called "obsolete and rigid conceptual thinking."[58] Unlike the Soviet publications on REC, Chinese publications do not give explicit estimates of battle casualties. As explained by Major General Dai Qingmin, then director of the PLA General Staff Department's Electronic Warfare and Electronic Countermeasures Department (Dianzi Duikang/Leida Bu, aka, the Fourth Department), the operational concepts are similar. However, the PLA expands on and modernizes REC doctrine by including "the integrated use of electronic warfare and computer network warfare . . . to paralyze an opponent's information systems."[59] These concepts are incorporated into military exercises, including "force-on-force" confrontation, in which a "red" unit, representing the PLA, is in confrontation with a "blue" unit, representing the enemy — an advanced military force capable of operating at the highest levels of information age warfare.[60]

INEW is a "systems-versus-systems" form of military confrontation on the 21st-century battlefield, dependent on space, cyber, and various information technologies.[61] One objective is to destroy the enemy's C4ISR, to blind the enemy and prevent enemy forces and commanders from communicating. But the PLA also wants to inflict battlefield casualties on an enemy force and to disrupt logistics, resupply, and personnel systems in the enemy's homeland so that combat losses cannot be restored and the deployed force cannot sustain battle. As Dai Qingmin states:

> after the information attack succeeds in suppressing the enemy, the enemy's plight of temporary 'blindness, deafness, and even paralysis' can be exploited for the quick organization of an 'information/firepower' assault.[62]

Dai advocates integrating "soft and hard attacks," employing information suppression, information warfare, and the firepower of missiles."[63]

Other cyber warfare strategists, such as Xu Rongsheng, chief of cyber security research at the Chinese Academy of Sciences, writes that in wartime, cyber warfare should be targeted to "disrupt and damage the networks of infrastructure facilities, such as power systems, telecommunications systems, and educational systems."[64] This approach is not something new in the PLA; the two PLA senior colonels who wrote the book, *Unrestricted Warfare*, introduced these concepts in 1999.[65] However, it took people like Dai Qingmin to formalize these ideas as military doctrine. As for those Western-based specialists on China and journalists who dismissed *Unrestricted Warfare* when it was published because it was written by two PLA political commissars, it should be noted that by 2011, one of them (Qiao Liang) was a major general at the PLAAF Command College.

Cyber Warfare.

PLA military thinkers include cyber warfare as part of information age warfare. Cyber warfare takes place in the electromagnetic spectrum; thus, there is a good deal of conceptual and operational overlap with traditional electronic warfare. These operations are designed to penetrate, exploit, and perhaps damage or sabotage, through electronic means, an adversary's "information systems and networks, computers and communications systems, and supporting infrastructures."[66] As outlined above, cyber operations are a component of INEW. Cyber operations also are closely linked to operations in space and to traditional forms of espionage or information-gathering. Indeed, most thinking about cyber warfare in China is "an extension of its traditional strategic thinking."[67]

China, like other states, is heavily involved in computer network operations. They are conducted primarily for five reasons:

1. To strengthen political and economic control in China;

2. To complement other forms of intelligence collection and gather economic, military, or technology intelligence and information;

3. To reconnoiter, map, and gather targeting information in foreign military, government, civil infrastructure, or corporate networks for later exploitation or attack;

4. To conduct the exploitation or attacks using the collected information; and,

5. To develop defenses or conduct defensive operations in the PLA (and China's) own cyber systems.[68]

With respect to strengthening political and economic control in China, skilled computer operators exploit computer systems to gain information about what political dissidents say, how they use the World Wide Web, and with whom they communicate. The organizations in China most likely to engage in these activities, however, are those responsible for internal security, repression, and control of the Chinese population, and control over the distribution of information. These are the Ministry of State Security, the Ministry of Public Security (MPS) and the system of Public Security Bureaus and People's Armed Police the MPS oversees, and organizations of the Communist Party such as the Central Propaganda Department.[69] Still, the PLA has the expertise to conduct such operations and is sometimes involved.[70]

The second type of malicious activity, essentially, is intelligence gathering designed to collect information of military, technical, scientific, or economic value. Gathering this intelligence information may speed the development and fielding of weapons in China and improve technology in sectors of China's industries while saving time and money in research and development; it often compromises valuable intellectual property. The organizations of the Chinese government with the missions and capabilities to conduct such activities span both military and civilian agencies in China, to include the PLA's Technical Reconnaissance Department (aka Signals Intelligence, or the Third Department), the Electronic Countermeasures and Electronic Countermeasures Department (aka the Fourth Department), the Ministry of State Security, and the state-owned companies in China's broad military-industrial complex.[71] Foreign business visitors to China with whom the author has had contact also have reported that in some localities Public Security Bureau personnel have cooperated with local authorities to gather information of economic value.

Reconnoitering, mapping, and gathering targeting information in foreign military, government, civil infrastructure, or corporate networks for later exploitation or attack may be the most dangerous cyber activity for American national security. This is where foreign intelligence or military services penetrate the computers that control our vital national infrastructure or our military, reconnoiter them electronically, and map or target nodes in the systems for future penetration or attack. Malicious code is often left behind to facilitate future entry. Regarding this third type of computer network penetration by China, the danger is that it could lead to a devastating computer attack. General James Cartwright, then commander of the U.S. Strategic Command (USSTRATCOM) and recently vice chairman of the Joint Chiefs of Staff, said, "I don't think the [United States] has gotten its head around the issue yet, but I think that we should start to consider that [effects] associated with a cyberattack could, in fact, be in the magnitude of a weapon of mass destruction."[72]

General Cartwright testified in 2007 before the U.S.-China Economic and Security Review Commission that China is actively engaging in cyber reconnaissance by probing the computer networks of U.S. Government agencies as well as private companies.[73] A denial-of-service attack by China has the potential to cause cataclysmic harm if conducted against the United States on a large scale; it could paralyze critical infrastructure or military command and control. China currently is thought by many analysts to have the world's largest denial-of-service capability.[74] In 2010 former National Security Agency director and director of National Intelligence Admiral Mike McConnell reinforced General Cartwright's admonition. He argued that just as during the Cold War, when the United States aimed to protect itself against nuclear attack, today it must endeavor to protect its "power grids, air and ground transportation, telecommunications, and water filtration systems" against the chaos that could result from successful cyber attacks.[75]

PLA Lieutenant General Liu Jixian, of the PLA's Academy of Military Science, writes that the PLA must develop asymmetrical capabilities against potential enemies, including space-based information support and networked-focused "soft attack."[76] Xu Rongsheng told a Chinese news reporter that:

> cyber warfare may be carried out in two ways. In wartimes, disrupt and damage the networks of infrastructure facilities, such as power systems, telecommunications systems, and education systems, in a country; or in military engagements, the cyber technology of the military forces can be turned into combat capabilities.[77]

Other military strategists from China's military academies and schools of warfare theory have suggested that the PLA ought to have the capability to alter information in military command-and-control or logistics systems to deceive U.S. forces on resupply missions or divert supplies. They say it also should be able to paralyze ports and airports by cyber or precision-weapon attacks on critical infrastructure.[78]

Although armed conflict between the United States and China is not a certainty, a cyber war already is under way, and besides penetrations for intelligence collection, there are regular attacks on the United States from sites in China.[79] PLA organizations are being trained and prepared in military doctrine to "expand the types of targets or objectives for armed conflict to command-and-control systems, communications systems and infrastructure."[80] Military strategist Wang Pufeng argues that "battlefield situational awareness is the core of information age warfare, which means that one must be able to destroy or jam the systems that are fundamental to [an adversary's] situational awareness."[81]

With regard to information warfare, Wang Bao-cun, one of the leading information warfare specialists in the Chinese military, reminds readers in China that "the global information grid and global command-and-control systems are fundamental to the American defense system, including global positioning satellites."[82] Other Chinese military publications suggest that to be successful in information age warfare, one's own military must have certain capabilities and must be able to interfere with an adversary's ability to exploit the results of "reconnaissance, thermal imaging, ballistic missile warning, and radar sensing."[83]

PLA Responsibilities and Cyber Penetrations, Exploitation, Espionage, and Warfare.

In terms of organizations, the PLA has divided responsibility for the conduct of electronic warfare, electronic defense, the collection of signals intelligence, and cyber operations. Notwithstanding the divided responsibilities, the Chinese military is well equipped and staffed to conduct such activities.[84]

The Third Department (Technical Reconnaissance Department, or *Jishu Zhencha Bu*) of the PLA's General Staff Department is responsible for technology reconnaissance, or signals collection, exploitation, and analysis, as well as communications security for the PLA.[85] The Third Department is often compared to the U.S. National Security Agency. Third Department intelligence officers are trained for various forms of electronic warfare and electronic espionage, but they apparently are also trained for similar activities in the realm of cyber operations.

The GSD's Fourth Department (Electronic Warfare and Electronic Countermeasures Department) is responsible for offensive electronic warfare and electronic countermeasures, such as the jamming and counter-jamming of various types of signals or communications.[86] Fourth Department personnel are skilled in electronic warfare and, according to a Northrop Grumman Corporation study, they are also probably charged with cyber penetrations.[87]

Given the Third Department's analytical and language capabilities, its personnel probably analyze and exploit the cyber information gathered in Fourth Department offensive actions. Each of China's military regions, as well as the PLAAF, PLAN, and Secondary Artillery Force (SAF), has assigned to its headquarters department at least one technical reconnaissance bureau subordinate to the Third Department that monitors foreign communications (and cyber activity).[88] In addition to the technical reconnaissance bureaus assigned to the military regions, Project 2049 Institute also documents more Third Department organizations, including three research institutes, four operational centers, and twelve operational bureaus that have a regional or functional orientation. This orientation can monitor phone, radio, satellite, or computer communications.[89] In the military regions, arms, and services, the technical research bureau alignment is:

- Beijing: 1
- Chengdu: 2
- Guangzhou: 1
- Jinan: 1
- Lanzhou: 2
- Nanjing: 2
- Shenyang: 1
- PLAAF: 3

- PLAN: 2
- SAF: 1[90]

Penetrations of U.S. Government agencies and defense contractors attributed to organizations in China had been detected for some time prior to the 2006 penetration. The National Aeronautics and Space Administration (NASA) suffered a series of other breaches attributed to Russia and China.[91] In *Time* magazine, one author opened the door on a series of Chinese breaches of U.S. Government and industry systems, introducing the efforts of a computer specialist who tracked breaches into Department of Energy systems — "following the e-trail to China."[92] But cyber penetrations traced back to China have plagued U.S. contractors and agencies for a year or so before this. A second *Time* article explained how a computer security analyst at a Department of Energy facility, Sandia National Laboratory, traced computer attacks and penetrations he detected to Guangdong Province.[93] Guangzhou Military Region, which includes Guangdong Province, is the site of another of the PLA's technical reconnaissance regiments.

It is difficult at times to distinguish the origin of a cyber attack or penetration, and attribution of a cyber operation is not always possible. The PLA may be acting through its Third or Fourth Departments or the Ministry of State Security may be acting. The origin might be from groups known as "patriotic hackers" (even if the PLA sometimes uses such groups), or it could be some company or organization in China engaged in electronic espionage.[94] That said, it is clear that in terms of its military doctrine and approaches to modern warfare — whether one calls it the informational, electromagnetic, or cyber domain of war — the PLA has embraced the medium.

Three former U.S. officials—Admiral McConnell; Michael Chertoff, former secretary of Homeland Security; and William Lynn, former deputy secretary of defense—said in a January 2012 *Wall Street Journal* opinion piece that "the Chinese government has a national policy of espionage in cyberspace. In fact, the Chinese are the world's most active and persistent practitioners of cyber espionage today." They pointed out in the same op-ed that "it is more efficient for the Chinese to steal innovations and intellectual property than to incur the cost and time of creating their own."[95]

Further, there are very clear linkages between China's traditional espionage efforts against military technologies and the targets of cyber espionage; the target sets are roughly the same. The U.S. Department of Justice has prosecuted a number of cases in which long-term Chinese agents working for defense companies sent back to China information on naval propulsion systems, naval electronic control systems, and stealth aircraft design. For the most part, these agents were convicted of economic espionage—violation of laws prohibiting the transfer of military-related information to China.[96] These are some of the same targets of Chinese cyber espionage.

In a 2011 report, the U.S. National Counterintelligence Executive (NCIX), an agency subordinate to the Directorate of National Intelligence, made the point that cyberspace is unique because it provides foreign intelligence "collectors with relative anonymity, facilitates the transfer of vast amounts of information, and makes it more difficult for victim and governments to assign blame by masking geographic locations."[97] The Directorate added that "Chinese actors are the world's most active and persistent perpetrators of economic espionage."[98] The Northrop Grumman Corporation, in a second report for the U.S. China Economic and Security Review Commission in 2012, suggests that when "highly technical defense engineering information, operational military data, or government policy analysis is the target of a cyber penetration from China," it probably is not the act of a criminal group.[99]

According to *The Washington Post*, China has managed to gather data on "more than two dozen major weapons systems" by breaching design data stored on computers.[100] The compromises reportedly included information on Patriot anti-missile and air defense systems, the V-22 *Osprey* aircraft, the Navy's Littoral Combat Ship and F/A-18 fighter, and the F-35 strike fighter, among other systems. One computer security firm, Mandiant, in a report on computer threats, reported that on average, companies go 243 days with attackers on their networks extracting information before detecting the activity.[101] In a report on a detailed investigation it conducted on one PLA Technical Reconnaissance Bureau unit based in Shanghai, the 61398 unit, Mandiant exposed the identities of several of the unit's soldiers involved in hacking U.S. systems.[102] These reports make it clear that besides a robust cyber and electronic warfare program, the PLA is supporting China's national defense, science, and technology development through cyber espionage.

Implications for the United States.

Considering how China is approaching war and the electromagnetic spectrum, the PLA is a world-class player in the cyber domain. China's cyber warriors have been able to penetrate computer systems, steal or manipulate data, and engage in electronic warfare on a global basis. The governments of the

United States, Australia, Japan, Germany, and Great Britain, to name a few, all have tracked cyber penetrations back to China. Much of this activity, given the nature of the defense-related systems that are being exploited, probably traces back to the PLA or goes to support defense production in China that helps the PLA. In addition, military publications in China make it clear that the PLA intends to use computer network operations in conflicts, along with integrated network electronic warfare.

PLA military planners and strategists are aware of the strengths and weaknesses in China's armed forces. There are limitations of how far the PLA, especially the PLA Army, can go in embracing information systems. PLA leaders understand that given the education base of many of the soldiers brought into the PLA, not every soldier will be able to function in a fully automated, computer-driven environment, nor will all soldiers be able to use or even have access to information systems. Still, the PLA is doing an excellent job of adapting these technologies to its forces. Moreover, China's military thinkers are developing their own doctrine and no longer depend on what they see happening in the U.S. Armed Forces or other militaries.

Two decades ago, in the wake of the U.S.-led coalition action in Iraq, the PLA realized that its military was not ready to take on a modern adversary that used networked C4ISR systems. For almost a decade, virtually all of the publications from PLA institutions quoted from or cited American military doctrine or manuals. Beginning in the mid-2000s, however, Chinese military thinkers began to develop indigenous doctrine on information systems and operations in the information age. Moreover, the PLA is fielding equipment, satellites, and communications systems to support information age operations.

The transition to information age operations has not reached down into every level of the PLA. In the SAC, it appears that full automation, information flows, and data flows only extend down to the missile-firing brigades.[103] But one can be sure that individual missile batteries can take advantage of limited data links and satellite-based timing and positioning data. In the PLAN, all of the major combat ships are net-worked and can share data. In the PLAAF, a majority of newer fighter aircraft are able to share data and be part of an information system managed by the PLA's own airborne early-warning aircraft. For the ground forces, automation and information age systems ap-pear to have penetrated down to the regimental level. By comparison, in the U.S. military, data exchange and situational awareness extend to squads and weapon crews—in some cases to individual Soldiers, Sailors, Marines or Airmen.

Some in the PLA believe that because the United States operates its forces over extended distances and depends on satellites and information systems, it has a weakness that can be exploited in conflict. They take comfort in the fact that the PLA does not depend as much on information sharing as does the U.S military. But what the PLA sees as one of its strengths is be-coming a weakness, because as Chinese forces depend more on information systems, they become more vul-nerable to interference, manipulation, and jamming.

In a notional assessment of how the PLA could exploit some of the weaknesses it sees in the U.S. de-pendence on information systems, researchers at the Northrop Grumman Corporation point out weak-nesses in the unclassified Internet systems used by the U.S. armed forces.[104] The U.S. military operates two forms of Internet protocols. The Secret Internet Protocol Router Network (SIPRNET) is part of the Defense Data Network, wich carries classified information. So far, Department of Defense (DoD) authorities do not believe that it has been penetrated. The Non-secure Internet Protocol Router Network (NIPRNET) carries sensitive, but unclassified, information. It has suffered a number of penetrations, many of which have been traced back to China. PLA publications consistently identify "U.S. logistics and C4ISR systems as the most important centers of gravity to target in a conflict."[105]

Unfortunately, vital logistical, personnel, and unit movement data are all carried on the nonsecure NIPRNET, and this network likely already has been mapped and penetrated by the PLA. This leaves the U.S. military open for exploitation by PLA forces in the event of a conflict. The PLA's emphasis on surprise, striking the enemy's center of gravity, and achieving information superiority means that in the event of a conflict, the PLA would likely initiate cyber and electronic warfare first, in the Asia-Pacific region, in the United States, and around the globe.

The PLA is not solely focused on information superiority in the cyber and electromagnetic spectrum. The General Political Department (GPD) — often in coordination with the Communist Party's International Liaison Department, its Propaganda Department, and military intelligence — also has modernized traditional propaganda and psychological operations for wars in the information age.

The United States also must think through how it intends to respond to the PLA's cyber operations. Defensive measures are important, but, increasingly, Congress and American companies are discussing the potential for offensive cyber operations designed to disrupt the networks of attackers and of "honeypots," or traps designed to lure in a hacker and either allow the attacker to extract bad information or to attack the hacker's system.

THE GENERAL POLITICAL DEPARTMENT AND INFORMATION OPERATIONS

The GPD is broadly responsible for Communist Party political and ideological training in the PLA. That covers a wide range of activities, from building troop morale through cultural shows, movies, the arts, and literature, to supporting museums and sports activities.[106] More importantly for the PLA and the Communist Party's internal security, the GPD serves as a personnel department, controlling dossiers on the political reliability of troops and officers, their training records, their security clearances, and their promotions. Internally, framing and molding public opinion through the media also falls to the GPD.[107] This department works closely with other Communist Party organizations, especially the International Liaison Department, the Propaganda Department, and the Organization Department—a central Chinese Communist Party organization that keeps track of the careers, advancement, and personnel dossiers of 70 million party members. In some cases, the GPD also works hand in hand with the PLA's Second Department (Military Intelligence).

As if the GPD's responsibilities were not broad enough, in 2003, the Communist Party's Central Committee and the Central Military Commission approved a new warfare concept for the PLA, the "three warfares" (*san zhong zhanfa*, generally abbreviated in Chinese as *san zhan*).[108] These are: (1) public opinion (media) warfare (*yulun zhan*); (2) psychological warfare (*xinli zhan*); and, (3) legal warfare (*falu zhan*).[109] The *PLA Daily* makes it clear that the three warfares doctrine is part of the PLA regulations for the conduct of "political work."[110] These three forms of political or information warfare can be performed in unison or separately, bringing into harmony the PLA's actions, the intent of the Communist Party, and the goals of the senior party leadership.

In the public opinion (or media) warfare effort, the PLA wants to influence both domestic and international public opinion in ways that build support for China's own military operations, while undermining any justification for an adversary who is taking actions counter to China's interests. In the conduct of psychological warfare, the PLA seeks to undermine the will of foreign civil populations and the enemy's ability to conduct combat operations. The PLA's psychological warfare goals are to demoralize both enemy military personnel and their countrymen at home. In legal warfare, the PLA seeks to use international law and domestic law to justify its own actions and assert its interests while it undermines the case for an adversary's actions. Legal warfare also tries to establish an argument by precedent in customary international law for China's position on an issue, when possible, by tying the matter to domestic law in China.[111]

Media (Public Opinion) Warfare.[112]

The idea in public-opinion warfare is to use all forms of media to influence both domestic and international public opinion on the rectitude of China's policies and actions. This includes newspapers, television, radio, social media, and the use of front organizations to convey messages to foreigners. Some of these activities are close to traditional propaganda operations, but others border on sophisticated deception operations or perception management.[113] In this sense, psychological warfare and media warfare have similarities.

Inside China, the PLA (and the Communist Party) want to guide public opinion to conform to party policy and objectives, and to ensure that workers, the intelligentsia, and the populace understand and embrace the party's line on matters. When aimed at Taiwan, media warfare efforts are designed to promote a "united front" between the citizens of Taiwan and the Chinese Communist Party on specific policy issues. The Communist Party's International Liaison Department and the GPD take the lead on Taiwan-related "united front" operations.

Internationally, media warfare efforts seek to counter the dominance (hegemony) of the Western media, while promoting the Communist Party's positions and views. These efforts are increasingly sophisticated and include such measures as inserting paid advertisements, written like news articles from Chinese publications, into American or other target foreign newspapers. In assessing this phenomenon, the U.S.-China Economic and Security Review Commission's 2011 report to Congress noted as an example that *China Daily*, a Communist Party–affiliated state-owned newspaper, paid for inserts in newspapers such as *The Washington Post* and *The New York Times*. The insert made the argument that one-party rule in China benefits both American and Chinese economic policies because it keeps harmony in Chinese society and keeps the steady production of goods at cheap prices for the U.S. economy.[114] The obvious objective of such advertising efforts is to attempt to discourage

Americans and their elected representatives from putting any emphasis on human rights in China.

China Central Television (CCTV) also has a number of stations operating overseas—broadcasting in the native language of the host country and in Chinese—carrying the targeted messages of the Chinese Communist Party. Often these broadcasts feature military shows depicting PLA exercises or training and military life, documentaries on China's military history, and features that highlight how the PLA is contributing to international peace and stability.

In the broader national realm of perception management and image shaping, an initiative by the Chinese Communist Party's United Front Work Department and the People's Republic of China (PRC) Ministry of Education to establish Confucius Institutes in foreign universities around the globe with funding from China is another sophisticated example of public opinion warfare that seeks to "use foreigners as a bridge" to promote and convey the message of the Chinese government and Communist Party. The institutes provide services, such as language and cultural instruction, on the campuses and in the communities where they are located. Some Americans, however, argue that Confucius Institutes are a way to engage in "soft power diplomacy," shaping opinions about China.[115]

Turning back to the PLA, one way the PLA contributes to perception management and image shaping is through senior officers' visits to other countries. Senior Chinese military leaders visiting the United States often use speeches and other forms of public diplomacy to develop themes consistent with China's defense and security interests. For example, when PLA General Chen Bingde, the chief of the General

Staff Department, delivered a speech in the United States in May 2011, he emphasized China's peaceful military tradition and the need for the United States to respect China's "core interests," such as its control over Taiwan.[116]

Another tactic in media warfare is to open for selective study the parts of the PLA that help deliver the message that the GPD and the Propaganda Department want delivered to foreign audiences while concealing other areas of PLA activity. This effort is designed to influence foreign observers' perceptions of China in a way that serves the purposes of the Communist Party and PLA. Domestically, the effort is designed to reinforce stability and Communist Party control around China.

One way that the GPD seeks to shape messages to foreigners is to sponsor visits to China by foreign groups with military affiliations, by military retirees, and by veterans groups — visits that include tours and contact with selected PLA personnel. The group that is often used as a proprietary organization for such activities is the China Association for International Friendly Contact (CAIFC). CAIFC is controlled by the GPD, but it also works closely with the Chinese Communist Party's International Liaison Department and the PLA's Military Intelligence Department in choosing its foreign targets. The author accompanied American groups invited or sponsored by CAIFC around China while he was a military attaché in the 1980s and 1990s. American targets included business people involved in heavy industry, electronics, aviation or defense, and leaders of veterans organizations. Invariably, on the Chinese side, the escorts came from the PLA's Military Intelligence Department.[117] The GPD maintains its own liaison department, subordinate to which is an intelligence bureau and the CAIFC.[118]

One recent propaganda and perception manage-ment initiative by the GPD and CAIFC involved a multiyear program to bring retired senior U.S. gener-als and admirals to China to meet with their retired PLA counterparts. In the Sanya Initiative, the meet-ings took place in the town of Sanya on Hainan Island, which has a climate similar to Hawaii's.[119] The lead for the Chinese side was General Xiong Guangkai, the former PLA chief of military intelligence.[120] The Sanya Initiative sought to soften the views of the U.S. mili-tary toward China and to influence the United States to reduce arms sales to Taiwan. The American partici-pants reportedly were encouraged to return home and meet with active military leaders, informing them of what they learned from the trip.

Media warfare, or public opinion warfare, gen-erally is targeted against both domestic and foreign audiences. Both audiences are influenced to adopt the main line from the Chinese Communist Party's Liai-son Department and GPD, sometimes acting through the latter's "loose" cover organization, CAIFC.

Psychological Warfare.

The second of the three forms of warfare has a longer history and primarily targets enemies and po-tential adversaries. Psychological warfare has been a central responsibility of the GPD since it was estab-lished. The PLA targeted Nationalist forces and the Japanese with psychological operations and also used them in the Korean War. The PLA believes that this form of warfare serves national defense. It targets the adversary's will to fight and is designed to lower the efficiency of enemy forces by creating dissent, disaf-fection, and dissatisfaction in their ranks.[121]

Historically in China, psychological operations involved the use of stratagem (*moulue*) and deception. In its psychological warfare operations, the PLA may target an enemy's values, its motivation for fighting, and, in peacetime or wartime, the logic of an adversary's foreign policy, security policy, or national decisions.[122] In this sense, psychological operations may target an adversary's civil populace and its leaders, as well as military personnel. Historically, psychological warfare operations also were intended to divide alliances. The PLA's objectives were to cause an adversary's allies to take a neutral position or become disaffected from the ally. This is still the focus of psychological operations today.

Quoting a former U.S. military attaché to China, one study sums up the means and methods of PLA psychological operations this way:

> Political signals may be sent through (1) public or private diplomacy at international organizations, such as the United Nations, and/or directly to other governments or persons; (2) the use of the Chinese and foreign media in official statements or opinion pieces written by influential persons; (3) nonmilitary actions, such as restrictions on travel or trade; or (4) by using military demonstrations, exercises, deployments, or tests, which do not involve the use of deadly force."[123]

In an analysis of the PLA's psychological warfare operations, Mark Stokes, a former U.S. Air Force attaché in China, quotes PLA strategist Yu Guohua, stating in *China Military Science* that the PLA:

> should sap the enemy's morale, disintegrate their will to fight, ignite the anti-war sentiment among citizens at home, heighten international and domestic conflict, weaken and sway the will to fight among its high level

decision makers, and in turn lessen their superiority in military strength.[124]

When the PLAN or the maritime or coastal patrol organizations in China stage incidents with foreign navies or fishing fleets, they are engaging in psychological operations. Such actions intimidate neighbors and other claimants to disputed territories, whether in the South China Sea or the East China Sea. By creating the impression that acting counter to China's interests or desires may cause China to use force, the PLA is able to dissuade or deter an adversary without resorting to combat.

In 1996, just before the presidential election in Taiwan, the PLA engaged in a major psychological warfare operation that, at the same time, was a display of military force and a warning to Taiwan not to go too far in moves toward democracy and independence. China did not want to see Lee Teng-hui become the first popularly elected president of Taiwan. Chinese military officers sought to meet with foreign military attachés in Beijing, including the author, to tell them that if the election went to Lee, it could mean immediate war. The PLA then conducted a series of military exercises off the Taiwan coast, firing ballistic missiles into preannounced impact zones at sea in the vicinity of the Taiwan Strait, conducting an amphibious exercise, and leading artillery practice. Before the exercises, the PLA announced to international shipping and aviation that certain areas of airspace and the sea would be danger zones because of the exercises and that all aircraft and ships should avoid them.[125] The PLA's choice of the impact zones, which bracketed Taiwan and the Taiwan Strait, had the effect of a temporary blockade or embargo of shipping and air travel to Taiwan.

Beijing's message to the people of Taiwan was, "Vote the wrong way, and you face a missile attack." To other countries, especially the United States, which has encouraged free elections in Taiwan, the message was that Taiwan was a major concern of China and if events went the wrong way, China would use military force.

Unfortunately for the PLA and the Communist Party leadership, this psychological warfare campaign backfired. On March 23, 1996, Lee became the first democratically elected president of Taiwan, with 54 percent of the vote. When the PLA missile-firing exercises began on March 8, 1996, President Bill Clinton announced that two U.S. carrier battle groups would be dispatched to the area around Taiwan. The carriers stayed in the area throughout the PLA exercises, which ended on March 25, 1996, after Taiwan's presidential election.[126]

The PLA sees psychological warfare as an integral part of the three warfares and modern information operations. Chinese legal scholars and members of the GPD also are active in what the PLA has named "legal warfare."

Preparation for War and Legal Warfare.

While students of warfare are thinking through Beijing's military doctrine in space, other Chinese strategists and legal scholars are engaged in an internal debate on how traditional ideas of sovereignty and the laws of war apply in space. The authoritative PLA book, *The Science of Military Strategy*, puts the legal aspects of the three warfares at the top of its means to "influence and restrict international law and the conduct of modern war." The PLA sees war as a struggle in the military, political, economic, diplomatic, and legal domains. For the PLA, "international law is a powerful weapon to expose the enemy, win over sympathy and support of the international community [for China], and to strive to gain the position of strategic initiative." *The Science of Military Strategy* further argues that one must:

> publicize one's own humanitarianism and reveal a lot of the war crimes committed by the opponent in violation of law so as to win over universal sympathy and support from the international community . . . to compel [the] opponent to bog down in isolation and passivity.[127]

Those who follow China's military development cannot ignore this area of PLA activity. Often the arguments are nuanced and ahead of international customary law in an effort to establish a legal precedent for China's actions or policies. With respect to actions in the global commons such as the seas, international airspace, outer space, and cyberspace, the legal warfare precedents and arguments in China imply that, before using military force, China would telegraph its intentions or justify its planned operations through public opinion operations or legal action.

One authoritative volume on the military legal system, *The New Revolution in Military Affairs and Building a Military Legal System* (*Xin Junshi Geming yu Junshi Fazhi Jianshe*), explored the importance of ensuring that the PLA sets out legal justifications for military actions in advance of any conflict.[128] The essays in this volume imply that even now, as debates take place in China over the range of sovereignty and China's authority in the South China Sea or in space, the GPD of the PLA is developing ways to justify in domestic law its potential military actions. The ultimate objective is to establish positions in domestic law that can be used to create a precedent or to have an impact in the future on international law and international opinion.

One reason for trying to ensure that the legal positions China seeks to take in the international arena are grounded in its domestic laws is that the PLA believes that this strengthens its legal arguments. In disputes with Japan and Southeast Asian nations, Beijing now refers to its 1992 Territorial Seas Law adopted by the National People's Congress as justification for its territorial claims in disputes.[129] The Territorial Seas Law extended sovereign claims over three million square miles of area in the East and South China Seas, demarcating it as Chinese territory on its maps. After that, when Chinese diplomats or legal representatives argued with officials of other nations, the domestic law was used as one of the justifications for the territorial claims. The 2005 Anti-Secession Law is another example of how domestic law is used by Beijing to justify potential military action in the future, in this case, against Taiwan.

To reiterate a point made in Chapter 7 of my book, *The Dragon Extends its Reach*, PLA officers argue that setting forth legal arguments for military action is important if a nation is to get international support — laying out the justification for legal warfare.[130] PLA legal preparation for a military campaign complements the use of military force.[131] The major PLA text explaining this rationale was validated at a military-wide August 2004 critique session.[132]

One aspect of this is not new; since the establishment of the PRC, the Communist Party leadership has been careful to establish *a casus belli* before taking military action. Such justification has been in legal or political terms. Prior to the entry of PLA troops into the Korean War, the PRC telegraphed its actions publicly with a declaration from Mao Zedong through the Indian government.[133] In the case of the 1962 Sino-Indian War, Chinese diplomats and military leaders carefully staked out their legal positions as early as 3 years before the conflict.[134] They did the same in 1969 with the Soviet Union and in 1979 prior to their attack on Vietnam. Thus, this concept of legal warfare has roots in China's diplomatic practice, which has been reinforced by its leaders' practice of modern war.

Zhang Shanxin and Pan Jiangang, two officers from the PLA's Xian Political Affairs College, believe that prior to any conflict, a nation must "muster public opinion in its favor" and conduct propaganda, psychological, and legal campaigns to ensure support for military action. They also suggest developing domestic law that justifies military action in international legal terms. These authors see this as a means of developing "comprehensive national power" and believe that the United States demonstrated the importance of such actions in the period before the 2003 attack on Iraq.[135]

Lu Hucheng and Zhang Yucheng, of the General Staff Department Political Department, classify "legal warfare" as a "special form of military operations" to be undertaken in preparation for a conflict. Lu and Zhang define these legal actions as "political preparation of the battlefield." They see legal arguments, propaganda, and international agreements worked in advance as justifying any necessary military action.[136]

Why is this concept of legal warfare important? In the recent past, Chinese scholars have set out their views on national sovereignty, sovereignty in space, and the need for "space control" in modern war.

These actions are consistent with this concept of legal warfare, and, should any conflict come about in space, they would provide the outlines of any PLA justification for military action. Monitoring the outlines of the PLA's legal warfare arguments is important. It is also critical that American military theorists interact with Chinese scholars and diplomats when possible as a means of limiting their ability to define the justifications for conflict and evolving international law on their own terms.

Justifying China's actions in international law and establishing positions in domestic law increasingly are important for the PLA as its strategists and planners think about space warfare. Officers in the GPD are setting out positions now that China can use in the future to justify attacks on foreign satellites or other space bodies, while other scholars in China deal with the limits and range of national sovereignty in the global commons. These legal warfare efforts are designed to establish positions in domestic and international law as a legal basis for military action or as a mean of limiting the freedom of action of other nations.[137]

China is developing its own ballistic missile defenses and has tested them against an incoming Chinese warhead. However, that does not mean China thinks the United States should field missile defenses.[138] The PLA is very aware of the deep political schisms in the United States over renewed nuclear testing, placing even defensive weapon systems in space, and the foreign basing of American forces. Debate rages in Congress, the scientific community, academia, and the policy community on these issues, with near-theological disputes taking place on issues of nuclear testing and ballistic missile defense. PLA legal warfare efforts are applied in these areas at academic conferences and in meetings with foreigners to reinforce agreement with Chinese positions. It is likely that the concept of legal warfare will be applied to these disputes as well.

The author was once invited to an international conference in England run by a group of British pacifists to debate issues related to arms control and space. The English group's partner from China was the Chinese Association for Peace and Disarmament. However, when I met the members of the Chinese delegation, I saw that four of them were either PLA officers or Ministry of State Security (MSS) officers I had met in China at other arms control events. In England, however, they operated under cover and identified themselves as "disarmament researchers."

China's "Peaceful Rise" Theory as a Case Study of the Three Warfares.

The PLA has managed to act globally in its media and propaganda campaigns and is increasingly able to do so in a nuanced way. The promulgation of China's "peaceful rise" as a new theory of international relations through a major propaganda campaign is a good example of a relatively successful effort designed to reassure China's neighbors and the world that China has peaceful intentions.[139]

In April 1998, four of China's national security scholars published a book discussing the theory of how China can rise peacefully as an international power without upsetting the international system.[140] (Earlier in their careers, some of these scholars were affiliated with the MSS.) The book examines how the rise of China as a world power (or superpower) can take place in such a way as to avoid war and another Cold War.[141] The authors began their work on the theory in 1994 and, through the China Philosophy Society, further researched the topic. With respect to Southeast Asia, one of the scholars, Yan Xuetong, explained that the strategists who had developed the theory of China's peaceful rise designed it as a response to the "China threat theory" advanced at the time by former Prime Minister and Minister Mentor Lee Kuan-yew of Singapore and Prime Minister Mahathir Mohamad of Malaysia.[142]

Later, the Central Communist Party School was the major actor in promulgating the peaceful rise theory internationally, an effort led by its executive vice president, Zheng Bijian. When he moved on to chair the China Reform Forum, a Communist Party–affiliated organization, Zheng continued to discuss the theory, and he advanced it at the Bo'ao Forum on Hainan Island in 2003.[143] The Bo'ao Forum for Asia is a nonprofit, nongovernmental organization (NGO) committed to regional economic integration in Asia that meets annually at its permanent site, Bo'ao, Hainan Island, China. In 2005, he published a version of his speech, "China's Peaceful Rise," in the magazine of the Council on Foreign Relations, *Foreign Affairs*.[144]

The peaceful rise theory is an interesting one. It suggests that China's rise as a great power is inevitable and that the different interests of a rising power and an existing superpower in the same region will create friction. Implicit, however, is the suggestion that it is up to the United States, as the lone superpower in the world, to accommodate China's rise.[145] Some American scholars have argued that the rise of great powers usually creates instability in the international system, particularly when those powers are nondemocratic states. The Americans cited the cases of Germany and Japan in the lead-up to the world wars as examples of the tension created by rising powers as they confront leading powers. Zheng responded with a new formulation:

> Our path is different from both the paths of Germany in World War I and Germany and Japan in World War II, when they tried to overhaul the world political landscape by way of aggressive wars. Our path is also to be different from that of the former U.S.S.R. [Union of Soviet Socialist Republics] during the reign of Brezhnev, which relied on a military bloc and arms race in order to compete with the United States for world supremacy.[146]

It was not only CCP intellectuals who put forth the formula. On December 10, 2003, Premier Wen Jiabao told an audience at Harvard University that, as a developing country, China would seek to rise peacefully as it resolves its natural resource and energy problems.[147] Sixteen days later, celebrating the 110th anniversary of Mao Zedong's birth, Hu Jintao told an audience that China would "develop along its own socialist course . . . and would follow a peaceful road to development."[148] Hu repeated the formulation on February 23, 2004, to a Politburo study meeting of senior CCP leaders, telling them that the peaceful development path would also follow a policy of self-reliance.[149] In addition, on March 14, 2004, Wen repeated the theory, telling a session of the National People's Congress that although China's peaceful rise would take a long time, it would not depart from the general interests of the world.[150]

The PLA and some in the Chinese Communist Party did not accept the peaceful rise formulation without some internal debate. At a meeting of senior PLAAF officers in May 2004, Jiang Zemin suggested that perhaps the formulation should be set aside, since the thesis potentially limited China's military development and modernization. His objection was both a manifestation of the friction between himself and Hu Jintao in the transfer of his power to Hu and a demonstration of genuine concern within the PLA that it could continue to modernize and strengthen.[151] In the end, after some period of debate, the Chinese Communist Party arrived at the position that "there is no contradiction between military modernization or military strength and China's peaceful rise."[152] China's policymakers in the PLA and the Chinese Communist Party see military development as complementing China's peaceful rise and feel that accommodating this rise requires an adjustment in attitude by the United States and Southeast Asian nations.[153]

There are unspoken elements in the peaceful rise formulation. An analogy that illustrates Beijing's attitude toward the peaceful rise debate is to imagine oneself walking down the middle of a sidewalk when another person comes unseen from around a corner and walks in your direction. That person's course does not deviate, as he or she expects you to shift your own course to accommodate his or hers. Failure to accommodate the new arrival could be interpreted as hostile and a direct challenge toward him or her. Moreover, since the path of the new arrival is not shifting, any failure to adjust your route could result in a clash. In discussions in Beijing and Shanghai in 2004 and 2005, some Chinese scholars made it clear to the author that the peaceful rise thesis implied that China expected other powers such as the United States to shift policy to accommodate China. However, in Southeast Asia, the campaign to promote the peaceful rise theory was relatively successful and won Beijing increased diplomatic influence.

The PLA part of the action is a series of military-to-military dialogues around Southeast Asia reassured China's neighbors of its peaceful intentions. Unfortunately for the PLA and the makers of China's foreign policy, a generally more aggressive policy on disputed territories, resource claims, and fishing rights in the South China Sea by the PLA and China's maritime surveillance authorities undermined several years of diplomatic effort.[154]

Responding to the Three Warfares.

Much of the PLA's campaign, whether in public opinion and media warfare or psychological warfare, depends on the fact that Westerners in general enjoy a free press. Thus, the PLA seems to believe that by constantly repeating its message in the Western press and in other forms of contact, it will be accepted. In China, there is no free press, and the PLA uses the controlled media there and Hong Kong's Communist-controlled media to deliver its message to the Chinese populace.

In the United States and other Western countries, the free press remains the major counter to China and the PLA's controlled messages. Most reporters are careful enough or cynical enough not to accept every message they are given; they check facts. Still, many Americans have no idea that the China Association for International Friendly Contact is controlled by an intelligence bureau under the PLA's GPD. Nor are most Americans or others in the West aware of the relationships among the Military Intelligence Department of the PLA, its GPD counterpart, and CAIFC. Public education, therefore, also is an excellent way to counter the PLA's efforts at public opinion, or media, and perception management; and psychological warfare.

The U.S. Government is working to counter China's internal propaganda campaigns through broadcasts on media outlets such as Voice of America or Radio Free Asia as a means to keep Chinese citizens informed. The Internet and social media also make it more difficult for the PLA to succeed with the type of controlled molding of public opinion it conducts. However, that does not stop the Chinese government from working to control social media and the Internet as well as to identify Internet activists.[155] This vying for public opinion and countering of propaganda is an example of one area in which the PLA has become more sophisticated, and its reach more global. In legal warfare, the PLA may be ahead. Few American legal or military scholars are engaging in arguments in legal journals that counter China's positions. At U.S. military schools and headquarters, there is no systematic effort to establish precedent or to counter some of the PLA's positions. International awareness of the PLA's strategy would be useful, making this another area in which public education could be the most effective counterbalance to propaganda.

ENDNOTES

1. This monograph was developed from Chapter 8 (Information Age Warfare and INEW) and Chapter 9 (The General Political Department and Information Operations) of Larry M. Wortzel, *The Dragon Extends its Reach: Chinese Military Power Goes Global*, Herndon, VA: Potomac Books, Inc., 2013. It is published with the permission of Potomac Books, Inc.

2. Wang Zhengde, ed., *Xinxi Duikang Lun* (*Information Confrontation Operations*), Beijing, China: Military Science Press, 2007, pp. 174-175, 199; Wang argues that confrontation in the electromagnetic spectrum is a major part of modern warfare space, the missile guidance, and command-and-control networks.

3. Zhang Yuliang, ed. *Zhanyi Xue (The Science of Military Campaigns)*, Beijing, China: National Defense University Press, 2006, p. 155.

4. Jeffrey T. Richelson, *The U.S. Intelligence Community*, 6th Ed., Boulder, CO: Westview, 2012, pp. 88–89.

5. Li Wuchao and Wang Yonggang, "Fen Jin de Bu Dai Yong bu Tingxie" ("The Pace of Progress Never Stops"). *Kongjun Bao (Air Force Daily)*, August 13, 2012, p. 2.

6. The Central Military Commission is the Chinese Communist Party's highest level military body. The chairman is Party General Secretary, and President Xi Jinping and the other members are the directors of the PLA departments; the army, navy, air force; and Second Artillery Corps. The General Staff Department (GSD) is one of four general departments of the PLA and is responsible for command and control of all forces. On the *qu dian* system, see Wortzel, *The Dragon Extends its Reach: Chinese Military Power Goes Global*, Herndon, VA: Potomac Books, Inc., 2013, pp. 37, 40, 134. Also see K. K. Nair, "China's Military Space Program," *Promoting Strategic and Missile Stability in Southern Asia*, Special Report 17, MIT/IPCS/CAPS Conference, March 28–29, 2006, New Delhi, India: Institute of Peace and Conflict Studies, 2006, pp. 9–10, available from *www.ipcs.org*.

7. Li Naiguo, *Xinxizhan Xinlun (A New Discussion on Information Warfare)*, Beijing, China: National Defense University Press, 2004, pp. 35–45.

8. "Laolao Bawo Guofang he Jundui Jianshe de Zhidao Fangzhen" ("Firmly Grasp the Important Guidelines for National Defense and Army Building"), *Jiefangjun Bao (PLA Daily)*, January 1, 2006, p. 1, available from *www.chinamil.com.cn/site1/zbxl/2006-01/01/content_374878.htm*.

9. Liu Mingfu, Cheng Gang, and Sun Xuefu, "Renmin Jundui Lishi shiming de You Yi Ci yu Shi Jujin" ("The Historic Missions of the People's Army Again Advances with the Times"), *PLA Daily*, December 8, 2005, p. 6.

10. Wu Zhu, Wang Lili, Hou Xiangyang, "Lianhe Jidong Biandui Zuozhan Tixi Wangluo Hua Maioshu" ("Using a Network to Describe Joint-task Fleet Battle System of Systems"), *Zhihui Kongzi yu Fangzhen* (*Command, Control, and Simulation*), Vol. 34, No. 4, August 2012, pp. 12-17.

11. Wang Zhengde, ed., *Jiedu Wangluo Zhongxin Zhan* (*Interpretation of Network-centric Warfare*), Beijing, China: National Defense Industries Press, 2004, p. 316.

12. Wang Xianhui, Yuan Jianquan, and Lu Junjie, "Zhencha Duikang Daji Yiti Hua Xitong Yanjiu" ("Reconnaissance, Electronic Warfare and Strike-integrated System"), *Hangtian Dianzi Duikang* (*Spaceflight Electronic Confrontation*), Vol. 25, No. 1, July 28, 2008, pp. 37–39.

13. Peng Guangqian and Yao Youzhi, eds. *The Science of Military Strategy*, Beijing, China: Military Science Press, 2005, p. 337.

14. *Ibid.*, p. 338.

15. See Dennis J. Blasko, *The Chinese Army Today: Tradition and Transformation in the 21st Century*, New York: Routledge, 2006, pp. 12-14. On PLA history, see Wortzel, *Dictionary of Contemporary Chinese History*, Westport, CN: Greenwood Press, 1999, pp. 132-136, 224-225, 258-259. See also Xiaobing Li, *History of the Modern Chinese Army*, Louisville, KY: University of Kentucky Press, 2007, pp. 94–112, 198–204, 250-259.

16. Ye Zheng, *Xinxihua Zuozhan Gailun* (*An Introduction to Informationalized Operations*), Beijing, China: Military Science Press, 2007, pp. 17–18.

17. Shen Weiguang, Jie Xijiang, Ma Ji, and Li Jijun, eds., *Zhongguo Xinxi Zhan* (*China's Information Warfare*), Beijing, China: Xinhua Press, 2005, pp. 2–3.

18. *Ibid.*, pp. 86–87. The authors seems to adapt the formulation used by the United States. See National Security Agency, "Global Information Grid," November 14, 2008, available from *www.nsa.gov/ia/programs/global_information_grid/index.shtml*.

19. *Ibid.*, p. 122.

20. *Ibid.*

21. This refers to the Communications Department of the General Staff Department, or *Zongcanmoubu Tongxinbu.* See Tongxinbo, "Zhanqu Xinxi Hua Jianshe Chubu Gouxiang" ("The Initial Concept of Theater Informatization Efforts"), *Junshi Xueshu* (*Military Art*), No. 7, July 1, 2004, p. 20.

22. *Ibid.*, p. 21.

23. *Ibid.*, p. 20.

24. *Ibid.*, p. 126.

25. Wang Yeming, "Zhiming Diqiu: Rang Weilai Zhanchang Geng 'Touming'" ("Smart Planet Makes Future Battlefields More 'Transparent'"), *PLA Daily*, December 16, 2010, p. 12.

26. Shen *et al.*, *Zhongguo Xinxi Zhan*, pp. 122, 126.

27. Ye *et al.*, *Xinxi Hua Zuozhan Gailun*, p. 19.

28. *Ibid.*, p. 23.

29. Wei Yufu and Zhao Xiaosong, *Junshi Xinxi Youshi Lun* (*Theory of Military Information Superiority*), Beijing, China: National Defense University Press, 2008, pp. 249–251.

30. Shen *et al.*, *Zhongguo Xinxi Zhan*, pp. 227–229.

31. Dai Qingmin, "Lun Duoqu Zhi Xinxi Quan" ("On Seizing Information Supremacy"), *Zhongguo Junshi Kexue* (*China Military Science*), Vol. 16, No. 2, April 2002, pp. 11–13. Also see Dai Qingmin, *Wangdian Yiti zhan Yinlun* (*Introduction to Integrated Network and Electronic Warfare*), Beijing, China: PLA Press, 2002, pp. 112–117.

32. Minnie Chan, "PLA Eyes Talent Pool to Expand Capability," *South China Morning Post*, April 20, 2011, available from *www.scmp.com/portal/site/SCMP/menuitem.2af62ecb329d3d7733492*

d9253a0a0a0/?vgnextoid=f0d7cc9cc2e6f210VgnVCM100000360a0a0a RCRD&ss=china&s=news.

33. Tongxinbu, "Zhanqu Xinxi Hua Jianshe Chubu Gouxiang," p. 22.

34. The Chinese term for INEW is *wangdian yiti zhan*.

35. Ye *et al.*, *Xinxi Hua Zuozhan Gailun*, p. 229.

36. *Ibid.*, p. 231.

37. David G. Chizum, *Soviet Radioelectronic Combat*, Boulder, CO: Westview, 1985, pp. 3-4; Department of Defense, *Soviet Military Power: Prospects for Change – 1989*, Washington, DC: Department of Defense, 1989; and David R. Beachley, "Soviet Radio-Electronic Combat in World War II," *Military Review*, Vol. 61, No. 3, March 1981, pp. 66-72. See also David M. Glantz, *Soviet Military Operational Art: In Pursuit of Deep Battle*, London, United Kingdom (UK): Cass, 1991, pp. 295, especially Chapter 5.

38. Dai, "Lun Wangdian Yiti Zhan," p. 113.

39. Wang Chang-Ho, *Chueh-chi I Tong Ya: Chu-chiao Shin Shih-chi Chieh Fang Chun (East Asia Rising: Focus on the People's Liberation Army in the New Century)*, Taipei, Taiwan: LiveABC Interactive Corp., 2009, pp. 219-20. Because this study originated in Taiwan, which uses the Wade-Giles transliteration system, the Chinese is rendered in Wade-Giles rather than pinyin. A similar point is made in Wang Wowen, "Chuan Tou Xinxihua Zhanzheng 'Mi Wu' de Li Qi" ("Sharp Weapons for Penetrating the 'Dense Fog' of Information Warfare"), *PLA Daily*, May 16, 2006, p. 11.

40. Wang Zhengde, ed., *Jiedu Wangluo Zhongxin Zhan (Interpretation of Network-Centric Warfare)*, Beijing, China: National Defense Industries Press, 2004, pp. 316-318.

41. Timothy L. Thomas, *The Dragon's Quantum Leap: Transforming from a Mechanized to an Informatized Force*, Fort Leavenworth, KS: U.S. Army Foreign Military Studies Office, 2009, pp. 38-39. See also Timothy L. Thomas, *Decoding the Virtual Dragon: Critical Evolutions in the Science and Philosophy of China's Informa-*

tion Operations and Military Strategy, Fort Leavenworth, KS: U.S. Army Foreign Military Studies Office, 2007; and Timothy L. Thomas, *Dragon Bytes: Chinese Information-War Theory and Practice*, Fort Leavenworth, KS: Foreign Military Studies Office, 2004.

42. Wang, *Jiedu Wangluo Zhongxin Zhan*, pp. 317-318. See also Thomas, *Dragon's Quantum Leap*, p. 39.

43. Ding Bangyu, ed., *Zuozhan Zhihui Xue* (*The Study of Command and Control Operations*), Beijing, China: Military Science Press, 2006, p. 4.

44. Wang, *Jiedu Wangluo Zhongxin Zhan*, p. 319.

45. Wang, *Xinxi Duikang Lun*, p. 174.

46. *Ibid.*, p. 199.

47. Defense Intelligence Agency, *Future Soviet Threat to U.S. Airbreathing Reconnaissance Platforms: A Special Defense Intelligence Estimate*, DDE-2623-1-86, Washington, DC: Defense Intelligence Agency, 1986, p. 4.

48. For studies on informatized operations or information age warfare in the PLA, see Che Yajun and Xue Xinglin, eds., *Zhanchang Huanjing yu Xinxihua Zhanzheng* (*The Battlefield Environment and Informatized Warfare*), Beijing, China: National Defense University Press, 2010; Shen *et al.*, *Zhongguo Xinxi Zhan*; and Si Laiyi, "Lun Xinxi Zuozhan Zhihui Kongzhi Jiben Yuanze" ("On Basic Principles for Command-and-Control Information Warfare"), in Military Science Editorial Group, *Wo Jun Xixi Zhan Wenti Yanjiu* (*Research on Questions about Information Warfare in the PLA*), Beijing, China: National Defense University Press, 1999.

49. Wang Xianhui, Yuan Jianquan, and Lu Junjie, "Zhencha Duikang Daji Yiti Hua Xitong Yanjiu" ("Reconnaissance, Electronic Warfare and Strike Integrated System"), *Hangtian Dianzi Duikang* (*Spaceflight Electronic Confrontation*), Vol. 25, No. 1, July 28, 2008, pp. 37-39.

50. Chizum, *Soviet Radioelectronic Combat*, Boulder, CO: Westview, 1985, pp. 3-4; Department of Defense, *Soviet Military Power:*

Prospects for Change – 1989; and Beachley, "Soviet Radio-Electronic Combat in World War II," *Military Review*, Vol. 61, No. 3, March 1981, pp. 66-72. See also Glantz, *Soviet Military Operational Art*, p. 295, especially chapter 5.

51. Extract from Chapter 1, *U.S. Army Field Manual (FM) 24-33, Communications Techniques: Electronic Counter-Countermeasures*, Washington, DC: HQ U.S. Department of the Army, July 17, 1990, available from *www.fas.org/irp/doddir/army/fm24-33/fm243_2.htm*.

52. *Ibid.*

53. Wang *et al.*, "Zhencha Duikang Daji Yiti Hua Xitong Yanjiu," p. 39.

54. Jeffery W. Long, *The Evolution of U.S. Army Doctrine: From Active Defense to AirLand Battle and Beyond*, Fort Leavenworth, KS: Command and General Staff College, 1991, available from *www.stormingmedia.us/47/4771/A477142.html*.

55. *Ibid.*

56. Peng and Yao, *Science of Military Strategy*, pp. 410-412; and Zhu Youwen, Feng Yi, and Xu Dechi, eds., *Gao Jishu Tiaojian Xia de Xinxi Zhan* (*Information Warfare under High Technology Conditions*), Beijing, China: Military Science Press, 1994, pp. 56-62.

57. Ye Zheng, An Introduction to Informationalized Operations, pp. 229-230.

58. Wang, *Jiedu Wangluo Zhongxin Zhan*, pp. 316-318. See also Wang *et al.*, "Zhencha Duikang Daji Yiti Hua Xitong Yanjiu," pp. 39-41.

59. Dai Qingmin, "Lun Duoqu Zhi Xinxi Quan," pp. 11-13. Also see Dai Qingmin, *Wangdian Yiti zhan Yinlun*, pp. 112-117.

60. Zhang Zhiwei, *Xiandai Huoli Zhan* (*Modern Firepower Warfare*), Beijing, China: National Defense Science and Technology Press, 2000.

61. Thomas, *Dragon Bytes*, p. 57.

62. Dai Qingmin, "Lun Duoqu Xinxi Quan," pp. 12-13.

63. *Ibid.*, p. 13.

64. Zhang Ying, "Zhanlue Pouxi: Zhonguo Bixu An Junshi Duikang Yuanze Yanjiu Wangge Zhan" ("Strategic Analysis: China Must Research Cyber Warfare According to the Principles of Military Confrontation"), *Dongfang Zaobao* (*Oriental Morning Post*), July 9, 2009, available from *www.dfdaily.com/node2/node23/node102/userobject1ai178135.shtml.*

65. See Qiao Liang and Wang Xiangsui, *Chaoxian Zhan* (*Unrestricted Warfare*), Beijing, China: PLA Arts and Literature Press, 1999.

66. U.S. Joint Chiefs of Staff, Office of the Chairman, *The National Military Strategy for Cyberspace Operations,* Washington, DC: Department of Defense, 2006, p. 5, available from *www.dod.gov/pubs/foi/ojcs/07-F-2105doc1.pdf,* cited in Robert Sheldon, "China's Great Firewall and Situational Awareness," *Strategic Insights,* Vol. 10, No. 1, Spring 2011, pp. 36-51.

67. Magnus Hjortdal, "China's Use of Cyber Warfare: Espionage Meets Strategic Deterrence," *Journal of Strategic Security,* Vol. 4, No. 2, 2011, p. 1.

68. Wortzel, "China's Approach to Cyber Operations: Implications for the United States," testimony before the Committee on Foreign Affairs, U.S. House of Representatives, hearing on "The Google Predicament: Transforming U.S. Cyberspace Policy to Advance Democracy, Security and Trade," March 10, 2010, available from *www.internationalrelations.house.gov/111/wor031010.pdf* and *www.uscc.gov/10_03_10_wortzel_statement.php.*

69. U.S.-China Economic and Security Review Commission (hereafter, USCC), *2009 Report to Congress,* Washington, DC: Government Printing Office, November 2009, pp. 289-309.

70. Wortzel, "China's Approach to Cyber Operations: Implications for the United States," March 10, 2010; and Bryan Krekel *et al.,* *Capability of the People's Republic of China to Conduct Cyber Warfare*

and Computer Network Exploitation, McLean, VA: Northrop Grumman Corp., 2009, available from *www.uscc.gov/.../NorthropGrumman_PRC_Cyber_ Paper_FINAL_Approved%Report_16Oct2009.pdf.*

71. Ellis L. Melvin, "A Study of the Chinese People's Liberation Army Military Region Headquarters Department Technical Reconnaissance Bureau," June 19, 2005. Melvin is a private citizen who served in the U.S. military in Taiwan and undertakes a great deal of personal research on PLA oroganizations in the Chinese language. He provided a copy of this study to the author. See also James Mulvenon, "PLA Computer Network Operations: Scenarios, Doctrine, Organizations, and Capability," Roy Kamphausen, David Lai, and Andrew Scobell, eds., *Beyond the Strait: PLA Missions Other than Taiwan,* Carlisle, PA: Strategic Studies Institute, U.S. Army War College, 2009; Wang, *Jiedu Wangluo Zhongxin Zhan;* Wei Baofu and Zhao Xiaosong, *Junshi Xinxi Youxiu Lun* (*Theory of Military Information Superiority*), Beijing, China: National Defense University Press, 2008; and Larry Wortzel, "China Goes on the Cyber-Offensive," *Far Eastern Economic Review,* Vol. 172, Issue 1, January/February 2009, p. 56.

72. USCC, *2007 Report to Congress,* pp. 95-96.

73. *Ibid.*

74. Robert Marquand and Ben Arnoldy, "China's Hacking Skills in Spotlight," *The Seattle Times,* September 16, 2007.

75. Mike McConnell, "How to Win the Cyber-War We're Losing," *The Washington Post,* February 28, 2010, available from *www.washingtonpost.com/wp-dyn/content/article/2010/02/25/AR2010022502493.html.*

76. Liu Jixian, "Chuangxin he Fazhan Lianhe Zuozhan Yanjiu de Ruogan Wenti" ("Innovation and Development in the Research of Basic Issues of Joint Operations"), *Zhongguo Junshi Kexue* (*China Military Science*), Vol. 93, No. 3, March 2009, pp. 1-17.

77. Zhang Ying, "Zhanlue Pouxi: Zhonguo Bixu An Junshi Duikang Yuanze Yanjiu Wangge Zhan."

78. Min Zengfu, *Kongjun Junshi Sixiang Gailun,* Beijing, China: Military Science Press, 2006, pp. 175-76. See also Jiang Yamin, *Yuan Zhan (Long Distance Operations)* Beijing, China: Military Science Press, 2007, pp. 133-40.

79. Bryan Krekel *et al., Capability of the People's Republic of China to Conduct Cyber Warfare and Computer Network Exploitation.*

80. Zhao Erquan, "Lun Xinxihua Zhanzheng dui Wuzhuang Chongtu fa de Shenyaun Sixiang" ("A Discussion of Far-Reaching Thinking on Armed Conflict and Informatized Warfare"), Liu Jixian and Liu Zheng, eds., *Xin Junshi Geming yu Junshi Fazhi Jianshe (The New Revolution in Military Affairs and Building a Military Legal System),* Beijing, China: PLA Press, 2005, pp. 498-505.

81. Shen *et al., Zhongguo Xinxi Zhan,* pp. 82-83.

82. *Ibid.,* pp. 86-87.

83. Wei Yufu and Zhao Xiaosong, *Junshi Xinxi Youshi Lun,* pp. 249-251, 287-290.

84. Krekel *et al., Capability of the People's Republic of China,* pp. 30-50.

85. *Ibid.,* pp. 30-32.

86. *Ibid.*

87. Bryan Krekel, Patton Adams, and George Bakos, *Occupying the Information High Ground: Chinese Capabilities for Computer Network Operations and Cyber Espionage,* McLean, VA: Northrop Grumman Corporation, March 7, 2012, pp. 45-55, available from *www.uscc.gov/RFP/2012/USCC%20Report_Chinese_Capabilities-forComputer_NetworkOperationsandCyberEspionage.pdf#xml= www.dmssearch.gpo.gov/PdfHighlighter.aspx?DocId=41&Index=D%3a%5cWebsites%5cUseIndex%5cUSCC&HitCount=2&hits=1f+9d4b+.*

88. Melvin, "Study of the Chinese People's Liberation Army," pp. 1-2. See also *Directory of PRC Military Personalities,* 2008, pp. 18-19.

89. Mark A. Stokes, Jenny Lin, and L.C. Russell Hsiao, "The Chinese People's Liberation Army Signals Intelligence and Cyber Reconnaissance Infrastructure," Arlington, VA: Project 2049 Institute, November 11, 2011, available from *project2049.net/documents/ pla_third_department_sigint_cyber_stokes_lin_hsiao.pdf.*

90. Wortzel, "The Chinese Way of Cyber War: The PRC Boasts an Extensive Cyber Strategy for Espionage and Battlefield Dominance," *Defense Dossier*, Vol. 4, August 2012, p. 3, American Foreign Policy Council, available from *www.afpc.org/files/august 2012.pdf.*

91. Paul Rosenzweig, *The Alarming Trend of Cyber Security Breaches and Failures in the U.S. Government*, Washington, DC: The Heritage Foundation, Backgrounder No. 2695, May 24, 2012, available from *www.heritage.org/research/reports/2012/05/the-alarming-trend-of-cybersecurity-breaches-and-failures-in-the-us-government.* Also see Keith Epstein and Ben Elgin, "The Taking of NASA's Secrets," *BusinessWeek*, December 1, 2008, pp. 72-79.

92. Nathan Thornburgh, "Inside the Chinese Hack Attack," *Time*, August 25, 2005, available from *content.time.com/time/nation/ article/0,8599,1098371,00.html.*

93. Nathan Thornburgh, "The Invasion of the Chinese Cyberspies, and the Man Who Tried to Stop Them," *Time*, August 29, 2005, available from *www.time.com/time/printout/0,8816,1098961,00.html.*

94. Hjortdal, "China's Use of Cyber Warfare," pp. 1-24. See also Shane Harris, "China's Cyber Militia," *National Journal*, May 31, 2008, available from *www.nationaljournal.com/magazine/china-s-cyber-militia-20080531.*

95. Mike McConnell, Michael Chertoff, and William Lynn, "China's Cyber Thievery Is National Policy—and Must Be Challenged," *The Wall Street Journal*, January 27, 2012, available from *online.wsj.com/article/SB10001424052970203718504577178832338032176.html.*

96. Interested readers can explore these cases by searching out indictments on the Department of Justice website at *www.justice. gov/usao/.* Another excellent compendium of espionage cases in

the United States is maintained by the CI Centre, a Washington-based security education company, available from *www.cicentre.com/?page=asset_prc_cyber.*

97. Office of the National Counterintelligence Executive (hereafter, NCIX), *Foreign Spies Stealing US Economic Secrets in Cyberspace: Report to Congress on Foreign Economic Collection and Industrial Espionage, 2009-2011,* Washington, DC: NCIX, October 2011, p. 1.

98. *Ibid.,* p. i.

99. Krekel, Adams, and Bakos, *Occupying the Information High Ground,* p. 96.

100. Ellen Nakashima, "Confidential Report Lists U.S. Weapons System Designs Compromised by Chinese Cyberspies," *The Washington Post,* May 27, 2013, available from *articles.washingtonpost.com/2013-05-27/world/39554997_1_u-s-missile-defenses-weapons-combat-aircraft.*

101. Mandiant, *Trends: Attack the Security Gap: 2013 Threat Report,* available from *www.mandiant.com/news/release/mandiant-releases-annual-threat-report-on-advanced-targeted-attacks1/.*

102. Mandiant, *APT1: Exposing One of China's Cyber Espionage Units,* available from *intelreport.mandiant.com/Mandiant_APT1_Report.pdf.*

103. Huang Luwei, Bi Yiming, and Yang Jifeng, "Daodan Budui Wangge Zhongxin Zhan Wenti Yanjiu" ("Research on Problems of Network-Centric Warfare for the Missile Forces"), *Zhihui Kongzhi yu Fangzhen* (*Command, Control, and Simulation*), Vol. 28, No. 2, April 2006, pp. 18-21.

104. Krekel *et al., Occupying the Information High Ground,* pp. 27-43.

105. *Ibid.,* p. 31.

106. Larry Wortzel, "General Political Department and Evolution of Political Commissar System," in James Mulvenon, David

Finkelstein, and Andrew N. D. Yang, eds., *The People's Liberation Army as an Organization: Reference Volume 1.0,* Santa Monica, CA: Rand, 2002, pp. 229-233.

107. Liu Gaoping, *Yulun Zhan Zhishi Duben* (*Textbook on Media Warfare*), Beijing, China: National Defense University Press, 2005, pp. 83-100.

108. For an excellent discussion of the three warfares in an article about training in a group army in Shenyang Military Region, see Mei Yushen and Yan Yongfeng, "Shenyang Junqu Mou Jituanjun Lakai 'San Zhan' Xumu" ("A Certain Shenyang Military Region Group Army Opens the Curtain on 'Three Warfares'"), *Zhongguo Qingnian Bao* (*China Youth Daily*), July 17, 2004, available from *zqb.cyol.com/gb/zqb/2004-07/17/content_910023.htm*. See also Hou Baocheng, "Zhengzhi Gongzuo Weishenme Yao Jiaqiang dui 'San Zhan' de Yan Jiu" ("The Need to Step Up the Study of 'Three Warfares' in Political Work"), *PLA Daily*, July 29, 2004, available from *www.pladaily.com.cn/gb/pladaily/2004/07/29/20040729001087. html*. There is a good summary of the three warfares in English in Timothy A. Walton, *China's Three Warfares,* Herndon, VA: Delex Systems, 2012.

109. Bhaskar Roy, "China: The Military and Leadership Power," South Asia Analysis Group, Paper No. 4052, September 20, 2010, available from *www.southasiaanalysis. org/%5Cpapers41%5Cpaper4052.html*.

110. Hou Baocheng, "Zhengzhi Gongzuo Weishenme Yao Jiaqiang dui 'San Zhan' de Yan Jiu."

111. See Peter Dutton, "Three Disputes and Three Objectives," *Naval War College Review*, Vol. 64, No. 4, Autumn 2011, pp. 43-67. See also Office of the Secretary of Defense, *Annual Report to Congress, 2011*, Washington, DC: Department of Defense, 2011, p. 26.

112. A direct translation of *yulun* is "public opinion"; thus, in many English translations, the term "public opinion warfare" is used. In some PLA translations of book titles and articles, however, it is called "media warfare."

113. In perception management, a nation or organization undertakes conscious actions to convey certain information or indicators of intent to foreign audiences to influence their emotions and reasoning. Perception management also may deny specific items of information to foreign audiences for the same reasons. The goal is to influence foreign public opinion, leaders, and intelligence systems, and to influence official assessment. The goal of perception management operations is often to mold foreign behavior in ways that favor the original actor's objectives. See Stephen Collins, "Mind Games," *NATO Review*, Summer 2003, available from *www.nato.int/docu/review/2003/issue2/english/art4.html*.

114. USCC, *2011 Report to Congress*, Washington, DC: Government Printing Office, November 2011, pp. 322-323.

115. Alan H. Yang and Michael Hsiao, "Confucious Institutes and the Question of China's Soft Power Diplomacy," *China Brief*, Vol. 12, No. 13, July 6, 2012, available from *www.jamestown.org/programs/chinabrief/single/?tx_ttnews%5Btt_news%5D=39592&cHash=ccbda5a33d17f73e50a7a3d92be5233b*. For a counterargument, see Peter Mattis, "Reexamining the Confucian Institutes," *The Diplomat: Diplomat Blogs*, August 2, 2012, available from *thediplomat.com/china-power/reexamining-the-confucian-institutes/*.

116. Chen Bingde, Speech Presented at the National Defense University of the United States, Washington, DC, May 20, 2011.

117. See Nicholas Eftimiades, *Chinese Intelligence Operations*, Annapolis, MD: Naval Institute Press, 1994, pp. 92-93.

118. David Shambaugh, *Modernizing China's Military: Progress, Problems and Prospects*, Berkeley, CA: University of California Press, 2002, pp. 131-136. See especially the chart on p. 135.

119. Bill Gertz, "China Using Retired U.S. Officers to Influence Policy," *The Washington Times*, February 7, 2012, available from *times247.com/articles/china-using-retired-u-s-officers-to-influence-policy*. See also Gertz, "Chinese Communists Influence U.S. Policy through Ex-Military Officials," *The Washington Free Beacon*, February 6, 2012, available from *freebeacon.com/chinese-government-influencing-policy-through-ex-military-officials/*. A copy of the

Sanya Initiative's own report on its 2008 program is available from *freebeacon.com/wp-content/uploads/2012/02/Sanya-Initiative-08-smaller.pdf*.

120. USCC, *2011 Report to Congress*, pp. 338-340, 352-353, notes 141, 142, 143.

121. Stokes, "The Chinese Joint Aerospace Campaign: Strategy, Doctrine, and Force Modernization," in Mulvenon and Finkelstein, *China's Revolution in Doctrinal Affairs*, pp. 271-274.

122. Zhu Wenquan and Chen Taiyi, *Xinxi Zuozhan* (*Information Operations*), Beijing, China: National Defense University Press, 1999, pp. 349-50; and Li Rongchang, Cheng Jian, and Zheng Lianqing, eds., *Kongtian Yiti Xinxi Zuozhan* (*Integrated Aerospace Information Operations*), Beijing, China: Academy of Military Science Press, 2003, pp. 156-162.

123. Walton, *China's Three Warfares*, p. 5. Walton cites personal communication with Dennis Blasko, author of *The Chinese Army Today*.

124. Stokes, "Chinese Joint Aerospace Campaign," p. 273.

125. *Ibid.*, pp. 272-273.

126. See Scobell, *Show of Force: The PLA and the 1995-1996 Taiwan Strait Crisis*, Stanford, CA: Asia-Pacific Research Center, January 1999, available from *iis-db.stanford.edu/pubs/10091/Scobell.pdf*.

127. Peng and Yao, *Science of Military Strategy*, p. 79.

128. Liu and Liu, *Xin Junshi Geming yu Junshi Fazhi Jianshe*. See also Zheng Shenxia and Liu Yuan, eds. *Guofang he Jundui Jianshe Guanshe Luoshi Kexue Fazhan Guan Xuexi Tiyao* (*Study Materials for Completely Building the Military and National Defense*), Beijing, China: PLA Press, 2006, pp. 192-194.

129. Law of the People's Republic of China on the Territorial Sea and the Continuous Zone, adoption date, February 25, 1992, archived by the United Nations, available from *www.un.org/Depts/los/LEGISLATIONANDTREATIES/PDFFILES/CHN_1992_Law.*

pdf. For a discussion of how domestic laws are used by China to justify its position in international law, see Hyun-soo Kim, "The 1992 Chinese Territorial Sea Law in Light of the UN Convention," *International and Comparative Law Quarterly*, Vol. 43, No. 4, October 1994, pp. 894-904.

130. One of the most important case studies in the PLA text that the authors used to validate the concept was the U.S. action in the Security Council justifying its actions in Iraq in 2003 on UN Security Council Resolution 1368, 2001, "Threats to International Peace and Security Caused by Terrorist Acts, available from *daccess-dds-ny.un.org/doc/UNDOC/GEN/N01/533/82/PDF/N0153382.pdf?OpenElement*; and UNSC Resolution 1373, 2001, with the same title, available from *daccess-dds-ny.un.org/doc/UNDOC/GEN/N01/557/43/PDF/N0155743.pdf?OpenElement*. Also see Xu Ou and Tong Yunhe, "Cong Yilake Zhanzheng Kan Guoji Fa Zai Weilai Zhanzheng de Zuoyong" ("From the Standpoint of the Iraq War, Examining the Utility of International Law in Future Warfare"), in Liu and Liu, *Xin Junshi Geming yu Junshi Fazhi Jianshe*, pp. 475-479.

131. Zhang *et al.*, *Zhanyi Xue*, pp. 205-207.

132. Liu and Liu, *Xin Junshi Geming yu Junshi Fazhi Jianshe*, p. 581.

133. See Alexander L. George, *The Chinese Communist Army in Action: The Korean War and Its Aftermath,* New York: Columbia University Press, 1967.

134. See Cheng Feng and Wortzel, "PLA Operational Principles and Limited War: The Sino-Indian War of 1962," Mark A. Ryan, David M. Finklestein, and Michael A. McDevitt, eds., *Chinese Warfighting: The Experience of the PLA since 1949*, Armonk, NY: M. E. Sharpe, 2003, pp. 173-197.

135. Zhang Shanxin and Pan Jiangang, "Fazhizhan de Hanyi yu Yunyong" ("The Utility and Implications of Legal Warfare"), Liu and Liu, *Xin Junshi Geming yu Junshi Fazhi Jianshe*, pp. 428-434.

136. Le Hucheng and Zhang Yucheng, "Faluzhan Zai Junshi Douzheng Zhunbei Zhong de Diwei he Zuoyong" ("The Util-

ity and Position of Legal Warfare in the Preparation for Military Conflict"), Liu and Liu, *Xin Junshi Geming yu Junshi Fazhi Jianshe*, pp. 355-362. See also Liu Zhongshan, "Ziweiquan yu Zhuquan" ("Sovereignty and the Right of Self-Defense"), *Zhanlue yu Guanli* (*Strategy and Management*), No. 1, 2002, p. 50.

137. The concept of "lawfare," or using the international legal system to lay the ground for and to justify military operations, is discussed in Qiao and Wang, *Chaoxian Zhan*. When the book was first published and discussed in the United States, many American "China watchers" dismissed it because the two authors were senior colonels in the GPD of the PLA. Over the years, however, the concepts have been reinforced in other Chinese publications. Qiao Liang has been promoted to major general and as of 2010 was a professor at the PLAAF Command College. See Qiao Liang, "Meiguo Ren Wei he Er Zhan," p. 11.

138. Rajaswari Pillai Rajagopalan, "China's Missile Defense Test: Yet Annother Milestone?" *IDSA Comment*, Institute for Defence Studies and Analysis, February 1, 2010, available from *www.idsa.in/idsacomments/ChinasMissileDefenceTest_rprajagopalan_010210*.

139. State Council Information Office, *China's Peaceful Development Road*, Beijing, China: State Council Information Office, 2005, available from *www.chinadaily.com.cn/english.doc/2005-12/22/content_505678.htm*.

140. Yan Xuetong, Wang Zaibang, Li Zhongcheng, and Hou Ruoshi, eds. *Zhongguo Jueqi: Guoji Huanjing Pinggu* (*The International Environment for China's Peaceful Rise*), Tianjin, China: Tianjin People's Press, 1998.

141. *Ibid.*, p. 2.

142. *Ibid.*, pp. 234-235.

143. The concept can be found in a speech by Zheng Bijian archived at the Brookings Institution. See Zheng Bijian, *China's Peaceful Rise: Speeches of Zheng Bijian, 1997-2004*, Washington, DC: Brookings Institution, 2005, available from *www.brookings.edu/fp/events/20050616bijianlunch.pdf*. Also see Zheng Bijian, "Zhongguo

Heping Jueqi Fazhan Daolu You Liyu Zhong-Mei Guanxi" ("China's Peaceful Rise Is Conducive to the Sino-U.S. Relationship"), *Luntan Tongxun,* China Reform Forum Newsletter, September 28, 2004, pp. 3-6.

144. Zheng Bijian, "China's Peaceful Rise," *Foreign Affairs,* Tianjin Vol. 84, No. 5, Summer/Fall 2005, pp. 18-24.

145. Zheng Bijian, in discussion with author, Beijing, China, August 23, 2005.

146. The Center for International and Strategic Studies (CSIS) in Washington, DC, maintains a regular program of exchanges with the Central Communist Party School of China and its China Reform Forum. A compilation of Zheng Bijian's speeches on "China's peaceful rise" can be found on the CSIS website, available from *www.csis.org.* See also Zheng, "Zhongguo Heping Jueqi Fazhan Daolu You Liyu Zhong-Mei Guanxi," pp. 3-6.

147. "Remarks of Chinese Premier Wen Jiabao, 'Turning Your Eyes to China'," *Harvard University Gazette,* December 10, 2003, available from *www.news.harvard.edu/gazette/2003/12.11/10-wenspeech.html.*

148. Hu Jintao, speech in celebration of the 110th anniversary of Mao Zedong's birth, December 26, 2003, *ibid.*

149. *Ibid.*

150. *Ibid.*

151. PLA officers in discussion with author, May 2004 and August 2005.

152. Zheng Bijian, in discussion with author, August 23, 2005.

153. Wortzel, "China's Peaceful Rise."

154. USCC, *2011 Report to Congress,* pp. 166-172.

155. USCC, *2010 Annual Report to Congress,* Chapter 5, "China and the Internet," available from *www.uscc.gov/annual_report/2010/Chapter5_Section_1(page221).pdf.*

www.ingramcontent.com/pod-product-compliance
Lightning Source LLC
Chambersburg PA
CBHW072016290526
45787CB00013B/922